Rebuilding Families

Rebuilding Families

A Blueprint for Child Custody Team Evaluations

Pamela Langelier, Ph.D.

iUniverse, Inc.
New York   Bloomington

Rebuilding Families: A Blueprint for Child Custody Team Evaluations

iUniverse books may be ordered through booksellers or by contacting:

iUniverse
1663 Liberty Drive
Bloomington, IN 47403
www.iuniverse.com
1-800-Authors (1-800-288-4677)

ISBN: 978-1-4401-2948-3 (pbk)
ISBN: 978-1-4401-2949-0 (ebk)

Library of Congress Control Number: 2009925021

Printed in the United States of America

iUniverse rev. date: 5/4/2009

Contents

Foreword

I am fortunate to have been the first psychologist faculty member of two respected judicial colleges: The National College of Juvenile and Family Law in Reno, Nevada and the American Bar Association's affiliated National Judicial College at the University of Nevada. My teaching topics have been Child Abuse and Neglect and Child Custody Decision Making. I have given keynote speeches including one on Child Custody for the Association of Family and Conciliation Courts. As a Clinical Associate Professor of Psychiatry, at the University of Vermont, I co-founded the first Child Forensic Service in the country. Later, I founded the Vermont Family Forensic Institute in So. Burlington, Vermont that offered training on child custody evaluations and on child abuse. I have directed child custody team evaluations for over two decades in both university and private practice settings. What I propose in this book comes from my experience of doing hundreds of such custody evaluations, listening to judges who have been my judicial college students and from training child custody decision makers: psychologists, psychiatrists and social workers.

Each year thousands of children and their divorcing parents experience the loss of a known family life, and land in a divorce quagmire that occurs when the parents cannot agree about what is best for the children. The licensed professionals who help the court extricate these families from being stuck in litigation can be from a number of backgrounds.

I have learned that good child forensic teamwork spans many disciplines, yet we lack a common blueprint and a comprehensive team protocol for examining a shattered family with the award of child custody as the rebuilding beginning point. States' Statutes have guidelines for judges to consider (The Best Interests of the Child), but they vary by location. Psychologists and psychiatrists have aging ethical guidelines and some "Best Interests" criteria from the older Uniform Marriage and Divorce Act (UMDA 1987). In fact, there are no ethical guidelines for team evaluations performed by the psychologist or psychiatrist. A major oversight in my opinion. Therefore, the ethical guidelines of the professional's discipline prevail.

Judges consider certain guidelines when they are forced to be the architects of the broken home, but these statutes may not be the basis for the judge's findings of fact. The custody evaluation and the resulting expert testimony often impact judicial decisions. Many mental health professionals and parents do not know that 'Best Interests of the Child,' the usual reference for construction of a post divorce family, are legal constructs set by the legislature of the state where the case is heard. These are not psychological terms but legal ones. This book blends both by offering a ten point best interests outline on which to base the definition of Best Interests of the Child in a custody dispute. I call these 'Building Plans.'

While perhaps only 5% of divorce custody cases are decided by courts, this minority of course is the most bitter, challenging and complex of all divorces involving children. Caught in the center of the fury, the children struggle to adapt and wait for the fighting to stop. Rebuilding a family with the judge and lawyers, the mental health professionals are usually solo practitioners or court personnel with widely differing training and experience. For children and their parents, there can be a "luck of the draw" outcome. In fact, few if any, graduate programs in psychology, social work, law or medicine have courses on 'How to Rebuild Divorcing Families.' Yet many professionals are doing just that with 'expert' influence and what is decided usually is the final construction, an awesome power in the hands of a few.

I would like to share with you a protocol to aid in custody decision making that can be used in any state and referenced by judges, lawyers, parents, and child advocates who want to know what to expect where custody and visitation is to be decided by strangers. Some basic assumptions underlying the recommendations you will read are:

1. Two Heads are Better Then One! The task of conducting an evaluation of warring parents, their supporters and their offspring is difficult and demanding under the best of circumstances. No matter how detailed the blueprint for Best Interests of the Child happens to be, and no matter how carefully the evaluation may be planned, a protocol that elicits family dynamics is important. Using a two person Forensic Team (a psychologist and one other professional, for example) and an

informed child custody evaluation affords hope that a comprehensive, logical all out effort was made to evaluate and offer a plan for the distressed family.

2. In general people (parents, families and especially children) do better in anxiety provoking situations (a custody evaluation) when what to expect is made clear by members of a strong team of professionals. I am opposed to solo evaluators using tests as a "team mate" for child custody decisions. When it comes to helping restructure the future of a family, the team offers objective reassurance and depth of expertise.

3. Child/Adult forensic evaluators may not know what the well trained judge is using as a reference for fact finding when rebuilding a family. It is the state's Blueprint for Best Interests of the Child. If you are doing custody evaluations, you want to know what that means and how it can be used in a team format.

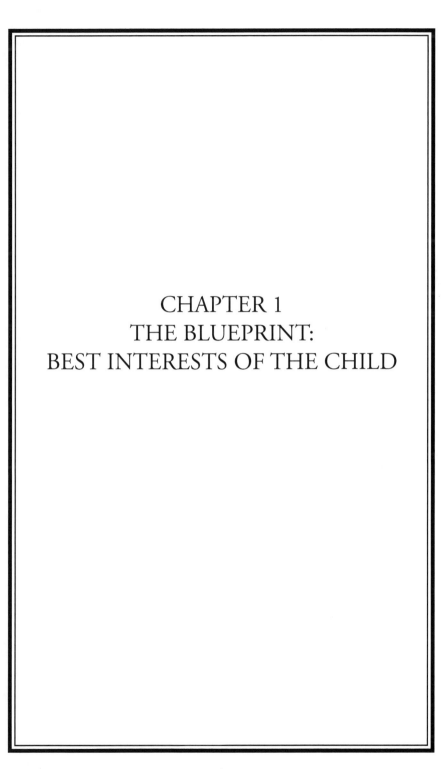

CHAPTER 1
THE BLUEPRINT:
BEST INTERESTS OF THE CHILD

The primary goal of a custody evaluation is to supply a reliable report that will help the court in its deliberations. This book sets forth the dual professional-team evaluation as most likely to bring a unique ability to elicit more helpful information than just a solo evaluator. Team evaluations are formidable when based upon the Child's Best Interests criteria as elaborated and refined in the blueprint proposed here. Family court judges that I have had the privilege of training at one of two Judicial Colleges, repeatedly stated that they wanted to know <u>how</u> evaluators arrived at their conclusions and recommendations. Transparent team decision making based on key criterion is recommended to address this need. New evaluators and even experienced mental health professionals may not be fully aware of The Best Interests of the Child criteria that are the corner stone of team fact finding in the protocol I propose.

The following ten criteria are a blend of legal and psychological points based on long established child custody statutes and forensic experience. States such as Florida, Vermont and Wisconsin have developed their 'blueprints' for awarding custody based on the seminal Uniform Marriage and Divorce Act (UMDA, 1987). Blueprint criteria 1 and 10 (Table 1.1) that address developmental needs of children and families are proposed to be special, new key factors, central to the issue of child custody decision making, drawing on knowledge from the disciplines of Psychology, Psychiatry, and Behavioral Science. A team evaluation is designed to uniquely address each of the following ten Best Interests of the Child, the polestar of custody awards.

Table 1.1

The Blueprint: Best Interests of the Child:

Key Factors to Consider in Child Custody Evaluations

1. The developmental needs and competency of the child – past, present, and future.

2. The demonstrated ability and capacity of each parent to meet the child's present and future developmental needs – psychological, social, and behavioral.

3. The relationship of the child with each parent and the demonstrated ability and capacity of each parent to provide the child with love, affection, and guidance.

4. The demonstrated ability and capacity of each parent to ensure that the child receives adequate food, clothing, housing, education, and health care to meet the child's other material and emotional needs, and to provide a suitable environment at home.

5. The quality and duration of the child's adjustment to housing, school, siblings and other relatives, friends, and community at the present time and the potential effect of any change on that adjustment.

6. The demonstrated ability and capacity of each parent to foster not only a positive or neutral relationship with the child and each other, but also frequent, continuing physical and verbal contact with other the parent, except where contact would result in harm to the child or to a parent.

7. The quality and duration of the child's relationship with the primary care providers, if appropriate, given the child's age, developmental needs, and competency.

8. The relationship of the child with any other significant

persons in the child's life including step-siblings, grandparents, stepparents, cousins, teachers, and child caretakers.

9. The demonstrated ability and capacity of the parents to communicate and cooperate with each other and to make joint decisions as to how parental rights and responsibilities toward the child are to be shared or divided.

10. The developmental needs of the family.

Evaluators should have clear knowledge of each criterion and should present their findings on each in a report format that is standardized and reasonable for the fact-based court. Few judges have had continuing education on all ten of these criteria; therefore, the team evaluation report with a psychologist and a psychiatrist or a social worker offers a comprehensive review of each for the court.

Typically, the most serious problem arising between judges and evaluators is over criterion or factor one of the blueprint: "The developmental needs of the child – past, present, and future." Not providing clear, useful information on this criterion is seen by judges as one of the primary failings of evaluators. Despite the central importance of criteria 1 and 10, evaluators whose expertise and primary concerns supposedly extend to the child's and family's developmental needs often overlook or fail to adequately explore these needs in their testimony and reports. Without appropriate useful information on these needs, judges lack a mental health expert's specialized input for making an informed custody decision.

As architects in the rebuilding of families, judges need to include in their findings of fact the Best Interests criteria as defined by state statute or as set forth in a blueprint based on those criteria, like the one shown in Table 1.1.

The forensic evaluation team as contractors are emphasized as organized, formidable, and capable of great depth and reliability. Sometimes the two-person multidisciplinary team approach, when structured according to the suggestions in the book, actually encourages resolution to the custody dispute prior to the court date. The old adage "Two heads are better than one" is powerful in helping to bring forth the dynamic functioning of the family before the breakdown (and afterwards) by having enough time and talent to elicit the best of the parties. Indeed a comprehensive examination of many stressed individuals (to decide the future of their children's families) requires and deserves the attention of more than one forensic evaluator.

For the novice, this book will help guide you through all stages of a custody evaluation, promoting good techniques and procedures such as the "Living Family Laboratory." You will be encouraged to form a team with a senior evaluator (or at least a second professional) who could lead the evaluation, schedule the work and make certain that all the necessary information is gathered before each, the novice and mentor, render opinions and reports. If team members are equal in experience, each undoubtedly brings a unique ability to elicit more helpful information than just a solo evaluator and the team avoids many common pitfalls.

Veteran forensic evaluators will enjoy the review of a seasoned, unique approach with examples and strategies that will serve to refresh, affirm and widen what they have learned over the years. The approach using a two-person team prevents burnout, omission of important points and examines both complex visitation issues and intricate child, adult and family development concerns. The team approach, as set forth in the text, attempts to bring out a full description of all involved family members. It allows for a variety of interviews with extra time to follow deeper into concerns and issues raised during the exam. In addition, the comprehensive model and subsequent testimony tips naturally include points of view from two experts looking at the same people for different reasons. One assesses a parent teaching the children new information while the other team member watches the siblings help the parent plan activities.

Team evaluations may even avoid a battle of the experts. The court recognizes this team effort as comprehensive, but no more costly than most solo evaluators because of the compact, intense two day Living Family Lab plan that is outlined in the Chapter 2.

The Blueprint used is known to both the legal and forensic professions, but less known to most general psychologists, psychiatrists and social workers, and is clearly explained and demonstrated. The Who, What, Where and How of teamwork is shown to be compelling, reassuring and based solely on the goal of helping the children be understood, adjust to visitation and be accepting of the outcome through carefully constructed recommendations. Real family dynamics are recreated in the offices of the team and seen at the same time by more than one expert in child development and adult and parenting models.

You will come to recognize that teamwork is a special, under utilized effort to collect data and inform the court of the child and family's profile in the heat of a major custody fight. The families that are team evaluated leave the office with the sense that the evaluation was fair, unbiased, extensive, focused and helpful. The evaluators often feel the same about their work using the unique model in the text. Remember, two sets of eyes and ears are better than one!

The Building Blocks: Salient Factors to Consider

When gathering data for your custody evaluation, let the ten Best Interests of the Child factors guide you. By doing so, you ensure that you will obtain the information you need to arrive at valid, useful conclusions and to make reasoned, appropriate recommendations. Below, each factor or criterion is reviewed in terms of what types of information are relevant; the information may apply to more than one.

1. *The developmental needs and competency of the child—past, present, and future.* Here you are seeking information about how the child is functioning in the cognitive/educational, social, emotional, behavioral, and interpersonal areas both at the present time and in the past. Looking for significant changes, whether positive or negative, in the child's development may relate to the divorce process.

For grade-schoolers, cognitive/educational functioning is reflected in the child's academic interests and achievements (grades, attendance record) as well as academic problems (learning disabilities, failure to advance to next grade). It is also reflected in the child's interest in extracurricular activities, such as clubs or sports, which becomes increasingly important with age. For preschoolers, an assessment of motor and language skills can give relevant cognitive information.

Social functioning includes the child's comfort with peers and ability to interact in an age-appropriate manner, information you may obtain for preschoolers in a play-group setting, where you need take into account the stage of play (e.g., parallel, cooperative). With grade-schoolers (children aged 5 to 12), ask about the child's activities with friends (how often and what kinds), popularity, team involvement, and attitude toward following game rules. For adolescents, information on the child's social group activities, perceptions of self in relation to peers, time spent with friends, and sexual development is important.

Emotional functioning is reflected in the child's age-appropriate comfort with separation from parents, autonomous activities, and individual interests, as well as mood, temperament, to include irritability and tantrums, and facility with transitions. An estimation of the child's self-esteem and self-concept is also relevant.

Behavioral functioning is reflected in the child's demonstrated skills. For preschoolers, these may be gross and fine motor skills, attainment of milestones, and the ability to adapt to new situations. For grade-schoolers, they may be coping skills such as the ability to manage anger, to follow rules, and to cooperate. Also relevant are the child's interests in projects, sports, and activities. With adolescents, you should also gather information on physical appearance and dress, involvement in peer activities, and anger management. Physical health is also important for all children and may be considered in relation to factor one or separately.

Interpersonal functioning, the final area, especially relates to parent-child interactions. What is the child's security of attachment? Are the child's concerns for a parent age appropriate or is the child overly concerned with adult issues such as money or sexuality? How do parent and child express affection? How do they communicate needs or desires? How does the child respond to this? How does the parent provide guidance and how does the child accept it? What is the child's response to discipline by the parent?

Table 1.2 Ivey in Coleman (1976) describes the key tasks and needs for persons at different developmental levels. In addition, it outlines expected problems when crises occur at different ages. Thinking about the stage of development for each family member when divorce takes place helps you both to identify the member's needs to be addressed in your evaluation and to arrive at appropriate recommendations. There is no definite, comprehensive, and unequivocal guide to how people change across the life cycle. But having table 1.2 for reference helps you estimate what may have happened or what may later happen to people and can guide your questioning.

Table 1.2
Stages of Human Development

Stage: Age	Tasks	Needs	Key Support Systems	Impact of Crises/ Neglect/Loss
Infancy: Birth–2 years	Strong bonding to other; sense of self; primitive reasoning; control of muscles	Security; to have needs fulfilled; stability; protection; empathy and positive regard	Family—parents, grandparents, relatives, siblings	Basic sense of trust or mistrust; failure to thrive or bond securely
Early Childhood: 2–4 years	Self-control; language; play and fantasy life; independent move-ment, morality	To learn from others; to have limits on behavior, protection from harm; to receive affection, empathy, and positive regard	Family—parents, grandparents, relatives, siblings	Lack of independent sense of self; doubt, fear, shame; bonding problems
Middle Childhood: 5–7 years	Self-identity; sex role; sense of right and self	Healthy role models; good teachers, protection, empathy, and positive regard	Family, parents, neighbors, school, peers, siblings	Independent sense of self or guilt about self's wishes, confusion
Late Childhood: 8–11 years	Social compe-tency, self-eval-uation, group identity	Safe school environment; social relationships; protection and support; empathy and positive regard	Family, parents, school, peers, siblings	Sense of inferiority or industry; school problems; sadness; addictions; anger; rebellion
Early Adolescence: 12–16 years	Ability to reason; peer group membership; athletic or intellectual interests	Strong support; protective rules; opportunities for judgment of self and others; empathy and positive regard	Family, peer group, school, parents, teachers	Sense of belonging or problems with social acceptance or adjustment; social isolation; rebellion; school failures; sadness; anger
Late Adolescence: 17–20 years	Independent living; work choices; moral behavior; ability to sustain intimacy; realistic thinking	To learn independ-ence; to take respon-sibility; to have self-esteem affirmed by family; to receive empathy and positive regard	Peers, siblings; school or work setting; family; community; Parents	Individual identity or lack or trust in self; confusion; addiction; rebellion; poor social adjustment; sadness; anger; early pregnancy

Table 1.2
Stages of Human Development (Cont'd.)

Late Middle Age: 62–70 years	Family; friendship; community	To make transition to retirement; to relocate interests, home	Community; spouse	Maintenance of physical strength through exercise or diminished physical strength; increase in pain
Elderly: 71–100 years	Extended family; friendship network; surrounding community	To cope with in-creased dependency on others; to evalu-ate own life; to deal with deaths of significant others and with own approaching death; to cope with child-ren's adult crises	Survival skills, given diminished physical resources; capacity to say good-bye and grieve	Sense of meaning and validation of worth or despair

2. *The demonstrated ability and capacity of each parent to meet the child's present and future developmental needs—psychological, social, and behavioral.*

From information gathered for factor one, you have created a picture of the child's and adult's functioning and present developmental needs, and you have a clearer sense of likely future needs. To assess the parents' relative abilities to meet child's needs, you could learn what each parent knows of the child's functioning in the above areas and how a parent uses this knowledge to meet the child's needs. This involves questioning the parent about the school, friends, and activities of the child and comparing this to reports from the child, teachers, and others. How does each parent react to the child's homework? How does a parent discipline the child? Is the parent too lenient or too strict? How does the parent view the other parent's relationship with the child?

3. *The relationship of the child with each parent and the demonstrated ability and capacity of each parent to provide the child with love, affection, and guidance.*

A parent's ability to provide nurturance and guidance is a key factor. What values and beliefs are taught in the home? Does the parent offer emotional warmth, support, and affection, and does s/he express these physically? Does the parent show a child-centered attitude when communicating with the child? Are the parent's responses generally helpful to the child? Is the parent willing to place the child's needs ahead of her or his own needs?

4. *The demonstrated ability and capacity of each parent to ensure that the child receives adequate food, clothing, housing, education, and health care, to meet the child's other material and emotional needs, and to provide a suitable environment at home.*

Here you'll gather information on the child's physical health and school functioning. What each parent says about the child's needs in these areas is important. A home visit is always helpful, especially when there is concern about possible neglect or housing standards. Take careful note of the cleanliness of the home, appearance, quality, and appropriateness of the child's clothing, hygiene of the child and parent, food in the refrigerator and cabinets, sleeping arrangements, prevalence of age-appropriate toys, and so on. If there are medical problems, how does a parent address them? For example, if the child suffers from asthma, is the parent able to differentiate asthmatic wheezing from congestion due to crying in an infant? Can the parent assess the situation and provide appropriate treatment? Does the parent smoke around the child or allow others to smoke in the home?

If the child has educational problems, what is each parent's understanding of them? Does this match what the school reports? How is the parent assisting the child? What is the parent's attitude about education? Does the parent have regular contact with the teacher and discuss how to approach educational problems? Here you'll find it useful not only to examine the child's report cards and attendance records but also to speak directly with the child's teachers and with other school personnel if appropriate.

5. *The quality and duration of the child's adjustment to housing, school, siblings and other relatives, friends, and community at the present time and the potential effect of any change on that adjustment.*

The information you've gathered about the child's emotional, social, and behavioral functioning is relevant here. What are the child's strengths and difficulties in dealing with the parental separation and divorce proceedings? Look for changes in the child's emotional and behavioral responses. Signs of stress and dysfunction as well as relief and improved functioning are important to consider. Exploring the child's support network beyond the parents gives you useful information about what is available to the child in each placement option. For example, with young children, will grandparents or consistent childcare providers still be available after the divorce? For grade-schoolers and adolescents, will peer networks and extracurricular activities important for the development of the child's self-confidence and identity still be present, or will they be disrupted?

To assess the likely effects of a change in the child's present living situation, you need to learn the child's perceptions, expectations, and anxieties. What does the child hope or expect life to be like in the next months or years? What does the child wish for? What is s/he afraid of?

6. *The demonstrated ability and capacity of each parent to foster not only a positive or neutral relationship with the child and each other but also frequent, continuing physical and verbal contact with the other parent, except where contact would result in harm to the child or to a parent.*

A parent's expressed attitude toward the child's relationship with the other parent has a significant impact on the future relationship between the other parent and child. Here you need to explore whether a parent can separate his/her own feelings about the other parent from the child's. Does the parent recognize the difference between his/her own feelings and the child's, or does the parent attribute those feelings to the child? Can the parent discuss the child's perspective when the child talks about his/her interaction with the other parent? Does the parent value the child's continued relationship with both parents? Can the parent accept differences in values between the parents? Can the parent identify ways to facilitate contact between the parents without further conflict?

Asking each parent why the child should respect the other parent can provide useful information on the parent's ability to separate his/her own feelings from the child's. When either or both parents cannot answer this question, you can anticipate continuing conflict between them to be played out through the child, along with possible visitation problems.

When one parent has been accused of child abuse or neglect, you should explore it. You should also explore the motivation of the accuser, the other parent. Is s/he making the accusation simply to gain in the custody dispute or out of genuine concern for child's safety? Here it is helpful to consult other people outside the immediate family but in a position to know, such as friends and relatives, teachers and other school personnel. It is important to assess a parent's ability to ensure the child's safety, ability to explain to the child at his/her level the reasons for supervised contact, and how the parent is coping with his/her own feelings about the alleged abuse.

7. *The quality and duration of the child's relationship with the primary care providers, if appropriate, given the child's age, developmental needs, and competency.*

Information on who does what is relevant here. Who feeds and bathes the child? Who toilet trained the child? Who goes to school conferences, sport activities, concerts, and so on with the child? Who attends to the medical care or stays home with the sick child? How much does each parent know about the child's activities? Does a parent know the names of important people in the child's life? Does the parent accept and support the child's interests and the role of others in the child's life? Is the parent aware of the child's daily routine or schedule?

Interviews and observation of parents and child will provide you with such information, as will other care providers' perceptions of the child's relationship with each parent and of parental behaviors. Evaluating the child's emotional attachment to each parent and other care providers is important here. To whom is the child most attached? Or is the attachment fairly equal?

8. *The relationship of the child with any other significant persons in the child's life, including stepsiblings, grandparents, stepparents, cousins, teachers, and child care providers.*

Information gathered here is similar to that gathered for factor 7 in relation to the other persons in the child's life. "Significant persons" may be grandparents, siblings, neighbors, teachers, or present partners of the parents. The quality of the child's interactions with these persons, the child's interest in their activities, and the child's support network are relevant factors. In addition, the presence of physical violence or aggression, high emotional parental or grandparental tension, and frequent conflict in the grandparental relationship should be considered. Interviews with these persons, observation of the child with these persons, and information from outside sources are all important here. (See chapter 5 for a discussion of grandparent visitation.)

9. *The demonstrated ability and capacity of the parents to communicate and cooperate with each other and to make joint decisions as to how parental rights and responsibilities toward the child are to be shared or divided.*

Here you need to assess the nature and extent of communication between the parents. Is it centered on the child or focused on old issues between themselves? What does each parent report telling the other? Does this include descriptions of the child's medical needs, social events, school problems? Does this match what the other parent reports hearing? Does it match information you have gathered from others?

What is a parent's attitude toward the other parent? Does the parent act respectfully to the other parent? What is the parent's perception of the other parent's strengths and weaknesses?

Can a parent give examples of situations where decisions were made? How did this occur, and was the parent satisfied with the outcome? If not, what did the parent do next? A history of the couple's relationship can provide relevant information. Interview each parent separately. Take a chronological history of the best and worse events they experienced together. In addition, observing the parents together without the child can provide you with further information about how the parents may act in front of the child. If one parent accuses the other of abuse or neglect, what are that parent's grounds, and how has the accused parent acted in relation to this knowledge?

10. *The developmental needs of the family.*

Families also go through stages of development as their members age, power relationships shift, and the demands on them change. For example, a family with young children may focus largely on meeting basic care needs. A family with teenagers will be more outwardly focused as the teens' peer activities take on greater importance. Consulting the latest research on the stages of the family life cycle will help you assess the family's developmental tasks at this time and those which may have been disrupted at the time of the parental separation. Most family therapy texts contain life cycle information as does the Internet.

Has the divorce disrupted the child's development? For example, is the young child anxious and unable to comfortably explore the world beyond the family? Has the grade-school child withdrawn from extracurricular activities or stopped bringing friends home? Was the adolescent child able to maintain an established peer network or to successfully create a new one? Or has s/he turned to substance abuse or delinquent behaviors? What has been each family member's way of coping, and has it been adaptive? Is each parent aware of the child's current developmental needs? Are parents able to continue to parent in a united way?

Chapter 2 elaborates on how to gather the above information through interviews, observation, psychological testing, and collateral sources. Although the information you obtain can be applied to several factors, it is helpful to concentrate first on what information you need to make a thorough assessment of each factor. As you do so, it is important to think about the strengths each family member brings to help the family cope with its challenges, and the limitations each brings to add to those challenges. These are central to factors that protect and disrupt the divorcing family.

Protective Factors

A good understanding of individual, couple, and family life cycles and developmental needs will help you find resiliency in the couple, the family, and the child. When assessing parental capacity, it is very important to identify and build on strengths and not to always focus on weaknesses. The healthy factors and follow-up questions listed in table 1.3 can guide you in your assessment.

Table 1.3

The Healthy Factors in Families

1. The rhythm of parent-child interactions.

    How involved (time and activities) is each parent and is this involvement on a daily, weekly, or monthly basis?

2. Historical profile of affection and guidance.

    What has the parent done (prior to this parental separation) to assist the child's development?

3. Predictability of a child and family's schedule.

    Who does what, when, and why? Is there a sleep, eat, school, play schedule that is predictable?

4. Good communication, respectful listening and feedback.

    Are understanding, respect, and compassion for the child's strengths in the parent? What specific instances can you cite?

5. Parental cooperation and low conflict.

    Does this exist in a way that encourages compromise, give-and-take? Do both parents cooperate with each other?

6. Adequate living standards and meeting the costs of raising a child.

    Is there enough money to pay the rent or mortgage and other bills, to feed and clothe the family? Will there be after the divorce is final?

7. Developmental expectations for each family member.

Is each person requested to do what is developmentally reasonable, or is the bar set too high? Should four-year-olds, for example, make their own lunch for day care?

Several qualities indicate positive parenting. The first is empathy and respect. Does a parent have not only empathy for the child and for the other parent but also respect? Does the parent <u>show</u> this empathy and respect?

The second is knowledge. A parent may have child development knowledge and may even be able to answer questions about it most appropriately, but does that parent also know the names of the child's teachers, dentist, doctor? What the child's report card said? It is easy for a parent to fake his/her way through most parenting tests or parental fitness questionnaires. To arrive at the truth, you must go beyond the "right" answers. Your interviews, information gathering, and observations must be thorough and in depth.

Reasonable rules are crucial to a child's development. They help build the child's self-esteem by letting him/her know what's okay to do and what's not. Self-esteem is probably the most valuable gift a parent can give a child regardless of the circumstances. Does a parent set and support such rules?

Next, clear generational roles are also crucial. Who does what? A single parent can find it very easy to lean on a child. As custody evaluator, you must assess whether a parent can maintain clear parent-child roles, or whether the parent will be more of a "leaner" —more of a "best friend"—than a parent. What's going on in the home now that the parents have separated? What historically went on? Does the child act like a parent, or like s/he is to blame?

An additional practical area to explore is availability. How much time does a parent have for the children? How much time is the parent willing to take for the children? Does a parent put the children first, <u>before</u> the career? These are important issues for dual career couples. The physical health of a parent may play a role in that parent's availability.

Judges like to see what "normal development" means in the evaluation reports they receive; they respect evaluators for what they know—and <u>show</u> that they know. As evaluator, you can thus take on the role of educator, too. You can attach pertinent, age-related information about the impact of divorce on children to your reports. Most children do recover from divorce within two to three years, after their parents and lives resettle. But if the parents—and especially the custodial parents—don't resettle, the children won't either.

The keys to a healthy divorce are like those to a healthy marriage: good communication and decision making; taking responsibility for personal adjustment; financial agreements that are fair; sensitive, empathetic adult parenting (no role reversals or using children for the adults' needs), equitable agreements on education, health, and involvement with the children. Mediation is a key ingredient in making divorce work as well as possible. Taking the initiative to think before speaking and cultivating patience also help. Support from family, school, community, and friends is invaluable to recover within a reasonable period of time (two to five years). Divorce is a major challenge, with stages of recovery, not unlike grieving a death or significant loss.

There are a number of factors in family life that have a disruptive effect on a child's development. Divorce in itself is disruptive, but problematic responses to divorce only add to that disruption: one parent blaming the other for everything, pursuing sole custody when shared custody has been suggested in mediation, promising to "get even." Continuous high conflict and tension between parents impair the child's ability to adjust. Torn between two parents, the child will try to accommodate both, becoming anxious or stressed by the parental war. The unique team evaluation attempts to help end the conflict for the child and promote the family's recovery from divorce.

Chapter 2
The Living Family Laboratory
Protocols and Team Interviews
The Standard Team Evaluation Protocol

Using the same careful procedures ensures comprehensive, quality information gathering, less influenced by referral sources, difficult clients or attorneys, or controversy. Set the format or protocol and hold to it.

When preparing to do any team custody evaluation, begin by reviewing your double protocol (two evaluators, two days) with your teammate and adjusting aspects of it according to the family constellation (children's ages, adults involved) and any accompanying issues such as embedded allegations of abuse/neglect, petitions by grandparents, medical or physical needs of family members, and particular background concerns. From this, you can develop a plan for which of you will interview whom, when, and with whom, what information you must gather, and if, when and why you will use psychological tests or parenting inventories.

You and your teammate can divide some tasks and duplicate others to look for consistencies and discrepancies in the information provided before, during and after the evaluation. Having a professional experienced in assessing child development is essential. Having both team members experienced in assessing adult personality is complementary to your team's understanding of family dynamics, past, present and future. Usually both evaluators (or a strong and experienced solo one) have expertise in both adult and child assessments. Two evaluators working together can complement each other's knowledge and maximize the evaluation process by jointly recreating a family's dynamics over an intense two consecutive days. The team can manage the opportunities for family members to talk with each other, develop questions among themselves as the hours wear on, and thus also regard the potential for family communication opportunities created by the two consecutive days of evaluation. Your procedures should result in gathering comprehensive information about all family members and their relationships. There are three key components of this type of custody evaluation: material or records from other sources, interviews, and observation. Testing is an adjunct and not always a key component to a team evaluation.

Protocol

The leader of the multidisciplinary team accepts a referral from the court and requests a letter with background information, from each attorney, to arrive one week prior to the first evaluation date. A letter is also sent to each adult scheduled for the evaluation with a request for all of the child's medical and school records to be brought to the evaluation. Any calls (faxes are not accepted nor are e-mails) are directed to the team leader. The leader reviews these letters and any enclosed documents that may provide crucial historical and position information about how long the dispute has been going on, what are the contentions, and whether parents have complied with prior agreements or any mediation.

The leader poses related questions to the team member prior to the onset of the first day's meeting and requests the answers at the end of each day. This attempts to keep past histories from biasing one evaluator's viewpoints. The team requests and reviews other pertinent medical and school records, physical and mental health, and child protective service's. Information from these records allows you to compare parent child and adult responses to your questions with facts on record and thus helps to assess the relevant self-related history and presentation of each person you interview. In addition it helps you assess the child's past and current functioning parent-child relationship, and any changes in either. The information you gather, consider and share before meeting clients, focuses your interviews on what needs to be addressed and understood.

The Family Laboratory and the Team Protocol

Observation gives you the opportunity to use your expertise (knowledge of individual and family dynamics) to gather objective data. The team evaluation over two or more consecutive days aims to promote, in effect, an intense "Living Family Laboratory" situation that elicits typical adjustments and coping skills by family members. For example, how does a parent relate to each of the children in this long (8-9 hours, two days in a row) high-stress situation? What parenting skills does the parent display? How does the parent handle noncompliance by the child? How does the parent interact with you or your teammate as evaluator? What characteristics of each parent are consistent or inconsistent across interactions? Observation can also give you information about a parent's daily living skills and attitudes toward others (Who is child-centered? Is anyone antagonistic toward one evaluator?) Directly observing parent-child interactions is critical to an adequate evaluation. How a stressed parent handles a tired child can tell you a great deal about parental capacity. Give that parent a second chance with the other team member, when the child is not tired, maybe on the second day in the morning. How does the second team member find the parent?

Observe each parent separately with the children in as neutral an environment as you can arrange. To increase objectivity, only one team member reviews all of the background on each parent, (and the parents know this) the other team member does not until the second day, unless there are special circumstances such as domestic violence findings. This is addressed later in Chapter 5. Sometimes you will want to see the grandparents together with the children, but this will be less often unless the grandparents are regular child-care providers or are requesting greater access. Grandparents are usually good child-care resources when parents are busy with team interviews. They also can be useful sources of information, biased or not.

Each member on separate days, asks either the parent or child to tell the children why they should respect the other parent. This turns the tables on them. When a parent states what is positive about the other parent, the children often show relief. This breaks the ice because the children may have expected to hear only what is wrong with the other parent. Indeed, if it is a polarized family, they may not at first believe Dad as he tells what is good about Mom. When asking a parent to remark on the good about the other parent, observe whether contempt is in the parent's face or if s/he can manage to say something genuinely respectful. This is an important marker in your assessment. Bitterness is corrosive. Which parent seems able to be balanced about the other parent's assets? Can stepparents do the same? Can the children's needs to like both parents be respected? Can the children also articulate unique positives about each parent or stepparent?

As another task, ask each parent to choose and to teach the children an unfamiliar, simple proverb. What's important here is twofold: whether a parent understands the proverb and how the parent responds to a frustrating, tense situation where s/he has unexpectedly been asked to be a teacher. Observe each parent's control, composure, reasoning, how spontaneous s/he can be, how cooperative the parent remains, whether s/he can talk at the child's level and so on. Many do an excellent job in this task. The family loses self-consciousness as it is engaged in the task. The team elicits original material that is genuine. Each team member, on different days, requests this activity.

Also, ask each parent and stepparent to teach a fact to each child. This will let you see in action a parent's ability to developmentally assess a child's needs and to teach the child new information at his/her level. For example does the parent try to teach a three-year-old daughter how to do math or how to tie her shoe? Allow the siblings to watch but not to coach because sometimes the other children know more about what to teach a sibling than the parents do. The children may laugh as they look on, which lightens the moment and takes the focus off them for a while. Many other tasks are possible. For example, you might ask the parent and child to build something with blocks or draw a picture together and then tell a story about either. The objective to observe the interaction and gather information on parental capacity as well as the parent-child relationship. Sibling and stepsibling bonding is usually evident as the day wears on and the children interact in various interviews.

Of great relevance is parental capacity. Parental capacity, in my opinion, is constructed of five variables: Empathy (respect); Knowledge (child developmental needs); Logical reasoning (rules); Clear roles (no reversal); Availability (physical and emotional) to the child. Many custody evaluators struggle to define this as do judges. Each team member considers all five variables and documents the findings in the final report. The Family Laboratory is designed to search for these salient criteria.

Team Interviews and the Protocol

Interviews are a primary fresh area of your information gathering. Each team member sees everyone in an intentionally planned complimentary variety of tasks and meetings. Accordingly, you must make sure these are cogent, focused, and broad in scope, and that your copious file notes are clear and well organized. Number every page from start to finish with a date on each page. Initial each page as part of the team file. Keep a detailed record of time and day and family members allocated to each activity.

An effective evaluation protocol includes extensive interviews with both evaluators, separately. Clients deserve enough time to tell two specialists what they think. Under pressure, the solo evaluator may take shortcuts with tests. The more face to face time, the better. Each evaluator sees the mother and father and other relevant adults for at least two and a half hours apiece on at least two separate days (or for five or six hours minimum). This will allow you to compare a parent's presentation on different days and times and can provide information about how the parent copes with stress. Having a teammate allows for someone else to help handle the unexpected during the evaluation. (A lawyer shows up in the waiting rooms or sends an inflammatory document about Dad's legal history). For just these reasons and more, the team encourages each parent to write the evaluators a letter within seven days after the final interview to state or further clarify his/her concerns. This gives the parent an additional opportunity to be heard when the parent has had time to think about what else could have been said and is offered a chance to do just that. Comparing team member impressions of the final letters from each parent is enlightening. The outcome is more likely to be seen as fair if not favorable.

A fair custody evaluation elicits much detail and you must keep separate, when interviewing each parent, both "factual" and observational information. Useful standard interview topics include each parent's social, couple, and vocational histories, the parent's perception of his/her relationship with the other parent and with the child, of the divorce, and of present stressors, and any other topic that allows you to assess parental capacity (see Chapter 1). Your questions might include: What are each child's needs? Can you describe a typical day with the children? Can you describe how each child and parent are adjusting to the breakup and what you plan to do to help each family member to recover? Why have you not been able to resolve custody on your own? Have you another custody evaluation planned?

It's important to identify the roles of each parent, adult family member, or older sibling. Who makes major family decisions? Who cooks the meals? Who gets the children off to school, doctor's appointments, or sports activities? Who knows the names of the teachers? How is the school bus ride? What is the name of the dentist? How much time does the child spend on the Internet?

Interview each child individually, the eldest first, and then together as a group. This allows a child to state anything the child wishes to say alone, but also to speak out as a sibling. Give each child tasks that allow the child to express fears, wishes, and information about relationships with parents in a non-threatening manner. Why are you here? Who explained this to you besides the team? Because loyalty issues are often primary for children, in your interviews you need to assist them in expressing themselves without creating loyalty conflicts. It's important to search for the positive aspects of the child's relationship with each parent. The negative history is always told. To assess the child's present level of distress and ways of coping with the divorce, ask some questions that are open ended: What are the best and worst things that have happened to each child? What are each child's daily routines and activities? What rules are there in each parent's home? How are they enforced? The children's answers can tell you about their lives and the effects of the separation on them. When you interview the children as a group, ask the siblings to talk about family activities. Who's the best at following rules, showing anger, or making others laugh, for example? Ask each child of at least age five to introduce a sibling and to say something special about the other child. To learn more about differences of opinion and family interactions, have all the children discuss what would make life better. Use humor to lighten the tension "would ice cream every day be a good idea?"

Giving "homework assignments" as part of the evaluation process to each parent will provide you information on the parent's ability to cooperate and attitude both toward the evaluation and toward the specific content of the assignment. For example, you might place each parent in a quiet room and ask each to write out what the best visitation plan would be regardless of whom has custody. Parents who have empathy for children can make themselves think both the unthinkable, namely, that they will not "win" custody, and what's best for the children regardless of who wins. Those who do have a hard time with objectivity often will not answer the question. Ask both parents to explain how they came up with their visitation plans. What will the other parent tell us are reasons you shouldn't have custody? What's your response? Why should you have custody, and why would shared custody not work? List the reasons. Such assignments can provide you with important focused information without the need to spend unnecessary amounts of time interviewing. Written in the parents' own words, their custody plans can also be reviewed when you're writing your report. For parents who do not read or who do not write well or at all, you need to allow more time to read or say your assignment questions to them and to listen to their answers.

Sample Interview Schedule

In the following two-day format, evaluator A, a forensic psychologist focuses on assessing certain family members; evaluator B, a child psychiatrist focuses on assessing both the children and parental capacity. This team evaluation offers a comprehensive overview of the family and helps make the most of two days of interviews. Potential bias by one evaluator is mitigated by the expressed feedback and information of the other.

Day 1

8:00 am   Orientation session with parents (includes informed

            consent and record release signing). Team leaders

            (Evaluators A + B) introduce schedule. The parents are

            seen separately as needed.

8:30 am   The child or children are met by the team for an

            orientation session as appropriate. The child care person is

            greeted.

8:45 am   Individual Parent Interviews Begin (Evaluator A).

            Commencement of assessments using parenting

            inventories and optional psychological testing (with all

            adults in separate rooms). Adults will continue to work on

these tasks (and others) throughout the afternoon when not in an interview.

9:00 am   Orientation session with stepparents or any other adults to be interviewed.

Team member (Evaluator B).

Team member (Evaluator A) continues to meet with each parent individually (social and vocational histories, relationship and personality issues, discussion of divorce and custody issues)

9:30 am   Evaluator B meets with each child individually to assess functioning, divorce stresses, and coping activities, decides if testing is needed.

Noon   Break. Team meeting. Lunch, exercise for children.

1:15 p.m.   Evaluator B meets with adults not seen in the morning. Evaluator A meets with children (as a group or individually).

3: pm   Evaluator A meets with adults as information and profiles begin to be developed.

Evaluator B meets, observes children with each parent and with each parent and their partner.

4:30 pm   Break for children with caretaker (snacks). Exercise.

5:45   "Homework" assignments given to adults (the best visitation plan) for the children not to be shared with any other party. Due the next morning.

6:00 pm   Evaluators meet to review information and plan for next

day.

Day 2

8:00 am   Team meeting. Any assessment results or salient

observations shared by each evaluator.

8:45 am   Evaluator A meets with children separately and as a group

and observers children with each parent and with each

parent's partner.

Evaluator B meets with each adult to assess parental

capacity and to understand their world view.

12:00-1:00 Team debriefing. Lunch break (plan which parent each

child will go with based on the present situation and

visitation orders).

1:00 pm   Continued questionnaire completion and testing for

children as needed

Evaluator A has second interview with each adult and may

see parents together.

Evaluator B has second interview with each child and/or

grandparents as necessary.

4:00   Snack break for children.

4:30 pm   Evaluator A may re-interview a child or an adult as

needed.

Evaluator B will re-interview stepparents or acting stepparents or grandparents.

6:00 pm   Joint parental conference with both evaluators (unless domestic violence has been alleged, then each parent scheduled and see separately.

Final homework request given (send a letter to the team within the next seven days).

6:30 pm   Family departs.

Evaluators meet about gathered information and start preliminary reports due within 14 days (seven days after any more information arrives from parents).

If more information is needed, follow up interviews may occur by phone. The team leader may do these. For some cases, such as high conflict families, a third day may be scheduled. Additional written comments are reviewed seven days after the final interview of the clients. Team reports are issued within 30 days of the final meeting. This efficient, time sensitive approach is enabled by the team protocol. The large volume of information is deftly managed by dividing the work at the end of the second day. Each team member creates a report with the Team Leader writing the opinion for the team.

One or both parents or "acting stepparents" may be hostile to the custody evaluation process, and one or both stepparents may be reluctant to be evaluated. This is not unexpected. All must be seen. No matter what you do, some parties in the evaluation may appear for the interviews against their will and may not want to cooperate fully. A prior custody evaluation, abuse allegations, old hurts, an extramarital affair (with the lover present), and other important situations, past or present, contribute to their resistance. At the very first meeting on the first hour of the first day, let each person (adult and child) know that, for anyone, the experience of being examined is stressful and that everyone will be subjected to the same sensitive protocols used with all referrals. Reviewing the day's schedule, maintaining a formal atmosphere while stating the obvious ("I know you feel tense") will help decrease hostility and anxiety. A planned structured team approach is encouraging for those who fear bias or not having a fair opportunity to be heard. Each adult should have a location of neutrality to relax in or to use for assigned tasks. Throughout the day "Living Family Lab," the children require a setting such as a waiting room with books, games or a quiet office for school work. A known childcare person (agreeable to both parents and required for the evaluation) is assigned to keep a watchful eye on the children.

Seeking information in a comprehensive, objective way involves careful scheduling after the team leader reads information supplied by the attorneys or the parties themselves that may signal a need for special consideration to keep some adults separated from each other. Different times for arrivals and departures on set schedules allows the team to minimize risk in the task. Cautious management of who is interviewed, when, where, and with whom is critical. Some of this is orchestrated prior to day one and some of it is planned at the end of that day for the second meetings on day two. Some planning evaluates as the day unfolds and unexpected information or behavior occurs. See Chapter 5 for more information on controversial issues. "Special considerations" are addressed later in this chapter.

Tests
When to Test and What to Consider

I cannot recommend any specialized tests for deciding child custody awards. There is no reliable data to support using tests to make custody choices, yet the use of psychological tests is a common component of many custody evaluations (Melton, 2007). Such tests have been said to allow you to assess a particular individual's strengths and weaknesses in a comprehensive, efficient manner and to compare them to those of the general population. They can permit you to confirm hunches. For example, considerable research indicates that important components of parenting for the child's healthy development are knowledge of children's needs, empathy for the child and consistent, reasonable rules. Although no tests can always reliably and accurately predict these qualities to be in daily interactions with children, when a parenting inventory is combined with interviews, observation, examples of how parents have assisted the child in the past and general feedback from school, the child or daycare personnel, perhaps a fuller picture emerges. Few parenting inventories can help you understand parents' styles and to assess their ability and capacity to meet the best interests of the child. However, an inventory might provide salient criteria for questions on a child raising issue. In particular, I have noticed that in families where incest or sexual abuse was alleged and validated, more likely than not, one or more of the evaluated adults has reported on the Adult Adolescent Parenting Inventory not being certain of correct sexual beliefs.

Some psychological tests have the advantage of objective, standardized scoring. This can reduce evaluator bias (or at least leave your evaluations less open to challenge). From standardized personality test results, you can pursue the questions raised. Team evaluators check each other for bias and rely on each other, not tests, to create fuller adult or child profiles. The solo practitioner or psychologist, as custody evaluator, relies on tests inevitably, to be "the team member." Not so in a team custody format.

Parents in child custody disputes frequently attempt to minimize problem areas and to present themselves in an overly positive manner. Information from tests—is not as important, as the "Living Family Lab" observational data—it helps you determine by unrehearsed process and action whether an individual is capable and reliable. A general sense of cognitive functioning can be obtained through educational records, yet for some adults (who appear to have intellectual or cognitive limitations), testing may be needed. Today, most tests can be obtained by most people, usually via the Internet. This is a challenge little discussed at present, but looming in the near future. How we work as evaluators must change now. You can avoid this issue by using few tests other than parenting questionnaires and perhaps a personality assessment instrument such as the MMPI. An effective psychologist can describe an MMPI profile of an evaluated client before seeing the scored results. In a team evaluation, this is routinely done to check for depth of knowledge and to stimulate team discussion.

Psychological tests are better at identifying overt psychopathologies than they are personality disorders (such as those exhibited by Borderline or Antisocial personalities). Thus, the test results of a manipulative individual may come out valid in the normal range, and you will be explaining why they do not match your clinical judgment.

Certainly psychological testing of children can give you information beyond what you learn directly from parents or others who may have an interest in the custody decision. It can identify and elucidate the child's present, specific developmental needs and aid in grasping future needs. Completed by each parent, child care provider and the other adult who now the child well, such as a grandparent or teacher, the Child Behavior Checklist developed by Achenbach (2007) will give you a broader, more complete picture of the child. Comparing two to six profiles on the same child (mom, dad, daycare, stepparents and school) can also counteract a parent's attempt to minimize a child's distress when the parent fears it will reflect poorly on his/her parenting abilities or when the parent simply misses the problems in the child. Likewise, some parents exaggerate a child's problems and going item by item or just using profile comparisons on such a test promotes a good sense of the child.

Be aware, however, that your interpretation of projective tests may be challenged by attorneys and should be, and must always be, viewed and presented in the context of other information gathered. Be prepared to cite research on reliability and validity of each. If you can't, don't use the test. In any event, testing should always be done only with the clear purpose of providing information relevant and valuable to understanding and furthering the best interests of the child. You need also to be attuned to ethical factors in the use of tests, including guidelines for disclosure (see American Psychological Association, 1997).

Finally, in deciding whether and when to test, ask yourself if testing will:

- Provide information not readily profiled by a team member who is a seasoned psychologist or psychiatrist?

- Significantly strengthen your presentation of a family profile?

- Enhance your understanding of the child or parents?

- Have relevant research literature available? For example, the MMPI has been widely used in child custody evaluations to assess parents' psychological adjustment, marital distress, and personality characteristics relevant to effective or abusive parenting (Pope, Butcher, & Seelen, 2006).

- Be a valid choice for clients with English as a second language?

- Require interval monitoring to ensure that procedural or vocabulary questions are answered? Or require you to read out loud a test item by item?

Special Considerations

For families where abuse and domestic violence are alleged, consider the following procedure:

- Set a special needs protocol for the team and stay with it.

- Keep adults separated in the office and outside by careful scheduling among the team.

- Respect any restraining orders or protection from abuse petitions.

- Schedule separate interviews of each family member, with the oldest child being interviewed last, the youngest first, and no parents on site during the children's evaluation. To avoid pressure, make sure parents and children do not mingle between interviews. Use two separate waiting rooms and each parent has "their office" where they must stay during the two-day assessment.

- Interview each parent separately, team members choosing who takes a full social, medical, and legal history, as well as a full history of the couple's relationship. Schedule the most hostile member last and see that s/he stays in a separate waiting room until then. No roaming of hallways is permitted. No cell phones can be used in the offices. There is always the same set of rules for all evaluations of custody. No text messaging of attorneys or faxing of documents is allowed on the premises of the evaluation

- Screen all parents for their own violence or victim histories. Ask them to describe their home environment, to recall their own parents and their best and worst life events; to describe any alleged harassment. Detail their concerns, if any, about the child's development as a result of witnessing violence in the home.

- After interviewing the siblings separately, interview them together as a group. Have them describe their home life and discuss information derived from your individual interviews and from your review of school reports. The children need to be at least age five for the joint interviews to be effective. Some children and adolescents may not cooperate. Some older children may act as parents or sentries, safeguarding the youngest or simply enforcing silence. Respect this, for the children may feel at risk when they leave the office. The team member for the children's evaluation confers with the team leader for a strategy on a case by case basis.

- Interview parents twice on the same day, keeping them apart between interviews and noting discrepancies between their separate statements about any incidents and between what they allege and what is on the record or found in the lawyers background letter. Team leader does this.

- After interviewing all the children, at your discretion as a clinician, hold a family meeting to expose the interaction patterns among family members. At some family meetings, the oldest child may appear to "mother" the youngest child and the disciplinarian for several of the children, while the mother, father, or both sit back and chaos reins. Some families have nannies or others as important child care members and they should be seen or interviewed by phone if a long distance from the office. Some nannies are seen in person as another adult in a parenting role. In one case of two celebrity parents, who had "the best" nanny was an issue. Ask each parent to teach each child something the child does not know but could learn, based on the child's age and developmental capacity. This may be the first time a child has had the parent teach him/her anything educational. Neglected children or those missing a parent absorb attention like a sponge. Some parents become anxious, refusing the task, At that point, I ask children to give hints or coach a tense parent. Whether in such a meeting or elsewhere, chaos, hostility, role reversal, lack of empathy, indifference, and calling parents by their first names can indicate hidden emotional barriers, which you should investigate.

- Intentionally reduce stress by increasing break time and decreasing continuous interview times as needed.

Collateral Contacts

You need to request permission from the parents to speak directly to third parties. Teachers, doctors, therapists, relative, neighbors, or other adults involved in the children's live can be of considerable help in clarifying and elaborating information gathered from records or interviews. Request that written statements from nonprofessionals, such as neighbors, be notarized before being sent to you. Document all phone calls, date, time, with whom and content. Read only solicited information; do not accept unsolicited CDs, tapes, documents. A team member is chosen to do outreach to these contacts.

Visits

Sometimes, when issues of safety, hygiene, space, or minimal standards for children are raised, you will choose on your own to make home visits as part of your evaluation. Although such visits can provide valuable information, if made by a team member, they can entail considerable expense for a family. Where the budget is tight, consider instead using graduate-level interns or residents (as extra team members) outfitted with checklists such as the one in Table 2.1.

Table 2.1
Child Home Visit Checklist For Team Member

1. Describe the physical structure and setting (geographic area, location of schools).

2. Describe each room and its contents, including kitchen.

3. Describe maintenance of property, furnishings, and general cleanliness.

4. Comment on each child's room, the home layout, toys, and play areas.

5. Comment on safety issues, health concerns, rules, and curfews.

6. Describe appearance, behavior, expressed thoughts, unusual physical or mental mannerisms, and leisure activities of each family member.

7. Describe school work, games, photographs, pets, and neighbors.

Summary

An effective evaluation is both art and science and can be, with the team approach, a strong structure for rebuilding a family. The list of procedures discussed in this chapter is by no means exhaustive. Evaluators should make best use of their clinical expertise to improve their information gathering and of their good judgment to adjust procedures to accommodate unexpected individual and family differences. What is important is that if as evaluators, you follow an effective, established team protocol including "A Living Family Laboratory," you will create for an in depth comprehensive answer to the referral question, who should receive custody and why. Whatever procedures you use, you should be familiar with your own strengths and weaknesses so that you can arrive at logical, consistent, well-reasoned and reasonably defended conclusions based on the Ten Best Interests of the Child Criterion. The team approach certainly ensures that such an evaluation is structured carefully in a reasonable period of time, no matter how complex the child custody referral may have been (or becomes) during the evaluation process.

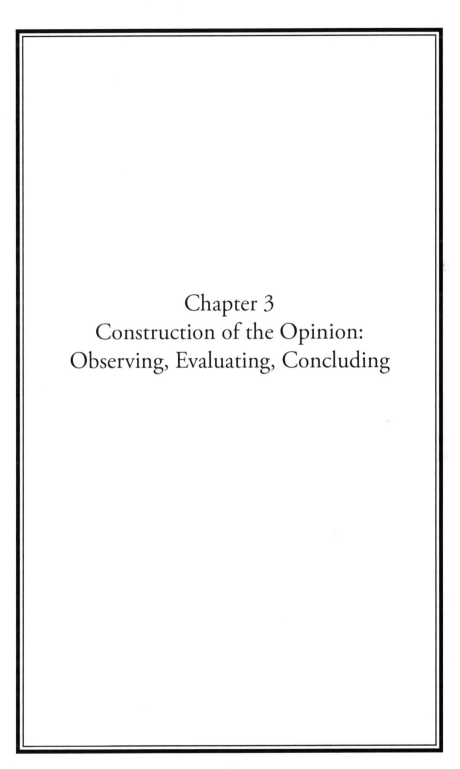

Chapter 3
Construction of the Opinion:
Observing, Evaluating, Concluding

Creating an Opinion

Organizing your thoughts and opinions in terms of the Best Interests of the Child criteria will help you arrive at your final conclusions and recommendations. Table 4.1 lists the evaluation procedures in terms of the 10 factors of the Best Interests blueprint, which should serve as the foundation for your report. Consider the information you have gathered and what you have observed with regard to each factor. How is each participant best described? Make the child come alive in your reports. Can parents provide equally well for the child? Where do their respective strengths and weaknesses lie? How do these bear on meeting the child's present and future developmental needs?

Table 3.1
Sample Organization of Data for Best Interests of the Child

Factor	Procedures
1. The developmental needs and competency of the child—past, present, and future.	• Interview with child alone at age five/six • Child's "Three Wishes" • Family drawing at age eight • Best and worst memories drawings • Description of peer activities • Description of school functioning • Child's self-perceptions • Piers-Harris Self-Concept Scale (optional) • Child Behavior checklist (CBCL) • Teacher Report Form (CBCL) • Youth Self-Report (YSR/CBCL) • Intellectual testing of child (optional) • Adolescent/Child Sentence completion (optional) • Felt board with felt figures • Interview with parent • Developmental Tests (optional) • Observation with siblings • Academic report cards requested • Academic testing reviewed • Individualized Education Plan (IEP consult with Special Ed) • Medical/mental health records of child reviewed ahead of meeting.

Factor	Procedures
2. The demonstrated ability and capacity of each parent to meet the child's present and future developmental needs— psychological, social, and behavioral.	• Interview with parent • Questions about child's school functioning • Questions about per activities • Questions about medical stats and care • Questions about interests • Checklists (AAPI or other parent inventories) • Parent's vocational, social histories • MMPI (optional) • Observation of parent and child • Task: Parent teaching child new information • Task: parenting teaching child proverb • Joint activity (picture, story) • Parent's discipline techniques • Health records of child reviewed with parent
3. The relationship of the child with each parent and the demonstrated ability and capacity of each parent to provide the child with love, affection, and guidance	• Interview of parents • Description of daily routine • Visitation/contact history • Observation of parent and child • Interview of child—activities with parent • Child Protective Services records (if applicable)

Factor	Procedures
4. The demonstrated ability and capacity of each parent to ensure that the child receives adequate food, clothing, housing, education, and health care, to meet the child's other material and emotional needs, and to provide a suitable environment at home.	• Child's medical records • Child's mental health records • Parental involvement with schoolwork • Parental involvement with activities • Parental understanding of educational needs • Parental understanding of medical needs • Phone interview with school personnel • Home visit when neglect is concern • Child's appearance • Parent's preparedness for child's needs during evaluation • History of domestic violence (Parent Impact Statement) • History of substance abuse • Parent's legal history • Intellectual testing (optional)
5. The quality and duration of the child's adjustment to housing, school, siblings and other relatives, friends, and community at the present time and the potential effect of any change on that adjustment.	• Interview with child • School reports • Changes in child's functioning with divorce dispute • Child's involvement with peers, community • Child's perceptions of current situation • Teacher (CBCL)

Rebuilding Families

Factor	Procedures
6. The demonstrated ability and capacity of each parent to foster not only a positive or neutral relationship with the child and each other but also frequent, continuing physical and verbal contact with the other parent, except where contact would result in harm to the child or to a parent.	• Visitation history • Report of what transpires in visits • Parent response to any abuse allegations • Parent ability to separate own and child's feelings about other parent • Parent's ability to take child's perspective • Task for parent to describe positive attributes about other parent
7. The quality and duration of the child's relationship with the primary care providers, given the child's age, developmental needs, and competency.	• History of family members' roles • How are basic care tasks divided • Parental involvement in school activities • Parental involvement in child's activities • Description of other adult as primary caregiver
8. The relationship of the child with any other significant persons in the child's life, including step-siblings, grandparents, stepparents, cousins, teachers, and child care providers.	• Child's perceptions of siblings • Child's perceptions of maternal and paternal relatives • Child's perceptions of parents' partners • Information from other relevant adults • Child's current relationship with step siblings

46

9. The demonstrated ability and capacity of the parents to communicate and cooperate with each other and to make joint decisions as to how parental rights and responsibilities toward the child are to be shared or divided.	• Observation of parents together by both team members • Reported conflicts around visitation arrangements • Parent demonstrated respect for other parent • History of marital conflict, communication.
10. The developmental needs of the family.	• Assess stage of family developmental needs • Children's ages • Children's expressed interests • Parental work or career demands • Ability for adolescent to maintain peer contacts • Parents' ability to parent in united way' • Ethnicity or cultural influences

Of critical importance is the likely stress and strengths entailed by any particular custody arrangement. Does the child have special medical or educational needs? If so, which parent can better provide for those requirements? For example, if a child is learning-disabled, with Attention Deficit Hyperactive Disorder, which school district has services available to meet the child's needs? Which parent is willing and able to participate in the educational planning processes and the homework help?

Each parent's present living situation is also important. Does the parent have another partner? Do they live together? What is the partner's parenting capacity and attitude toward the child and the other parent? How does the child interact with the partner and any children from this partner? How does the parent balance the demands of the new relationships with the child's needs?

Half of all highly contested custody battles involve some kind of electronic communications. Increasingly judges are asked to look at a parent's suitability to be the custodian of the children, based on copies of the hard drives of parents' computers. Nevertheless, your opinion needs to avoid this background data and concentrate on what you have found after considering all the reliable information. I have not allowed tapes, electronic files, nor other unsolicited information to be part of decision making. Data can be manipulated. Live observation is direct and immediate.

Exploring parental alienation and abuse allegations may help answer some of the above questions, especially when there are discrepancies between the information you've obtained, legal records, allegations, and the interactions you've observed (see "How to Interview High-Conflict Families" in Chapter 3).

It is also important to consider how a parent's personality, parenting style, and mental health bear on his/her parenting. If a parent has a history of violence, substance abuse, etc. you need to carefully weigh the evidence to assess the safety and well being of the child while with that parent. How a parent has complied with previous contentious issues, suggests how likely that parent is to comply with future visitation and custody arrangements based on your evaluation.

Where high conflict exists between parents, especially where mediation has failed or may, the frequent shifts between parental households that joint custody entails may be too stressful for the child and family. To increase the likelihood of continued contact between parents, the parent more able to foster that contact may be the better choice to have custody of the child. In high conflict situations, more than once, I have seen the "best" parent abandon the custody battle to remove the child from the war. It is a gesture of remarkable compassion.

Joint or Shared Custody.

By returning time and again to the Best Interests of the Child criteria, evaluators and judge are able to remain grounded in them and to formulate reasonable options for rebuilding families in complex situations. Balancing the children's right to live continuously under one roof and with their siblings, on the one hand, and each parent's right to be with them, on the other, has resulted in some complex scheduling. Shared custody is common among parents who, when divorcing, can come to agreements about the children. Whether or not parents request shared legal custody, however, you must consider it an option in terms of the Best Interests of the Child as defined by your state or set out in the Best Interests blueprint of this text. When the quality of the child's relationship with both parents is predominantly positive; when both parents demonstrate good parenting skills; are willing to care for the child, and have demonstrated they can separate their personal conflicts from their parental roles and cooperate with regard to the child; and especially when the child, being of "sufficient age and capability" (as defined by state law; some states have no such defined age), has expressed a preference for it, some form of shared custody may be a workable, beneficial option for the child.

Arguments for and against joint custody or shared parenting arrangements are listed in table 3.2 Review them carefully as you set about forming your opinion. Many courts award shared legal parenting, with one parent having sole physical custody and generous visitation awarded to the other parent.

Factors favoring joint custody include both parents being in support of it; parents residing within commuting distance of each other and having compatible work schedules; parents having similar lifestyles and similar philosophies on child rearing and discipline; and both parents being fit and willing to cooperate on matters concerning the child. Factors militating against joint custody include both parents being opposed to it; parents residing far apart or having incompatible work schedules; parents having significant disagreements on lifestyle and how to rear and discipline the child; a history of violence, addiction, child neglect or abuse, or significant mental or physical health issues on the part of either parent; and continuous high conflict between parents. The general criteria for a recommendation of joint custody are set out in Table 3.3

Table 3.2
Shared Joint Custody Arguments

	For	Against
1.	Children have opportunity to know and love each parent through realistic relationship, not just on weekends.	Joint custody creates instability for children and works less and less well as they grow older. They may remain caught in the fighting of parents vying for time.
2.	Both parents remain involved in lives of children	Children need sense of "finality," and so do parents—that is, divorce, loss.
3.	Both parents are often "equally fit," and both want children to have two parents.	Cooperation between the parents is needed but almost impossible to attain.
4.	Sole parenting burdens are relieved—time, money, energy, decision making.	Parental authority and discipline breaks down; there is absence of clear decision-making authority
5.	There is greater likelihood that grand-parents and extended family will remain involved and supportive in lives of children.	Manipulation of children by parents gets worse with joint custody arrangements.

6.	Joint custody decreases likelihood of default on child support and prevents some economic hardship.	Joint custody may take an exhausting toll on children.
7.	If parents can negotiate and compromise, they can avoid conflict	Divorce never ends with joint custody—children are in middle of continuing conflict.
8.	Shared parenting encourages parents to give up some opportunities and to put children first.	Odds of future problems increase—what happens if one parent moves or remarries?

Table 3.3
General Criteria for Shared or Joint Custody

1. Both parents have shown that they are committed to making joint custody work.

2. Both parents have shown that they clearly understand their respective roles in a joint custody plan and are willing and able to negotiate differences or participate in mediation.

3. Both parents have shown that they can put their child's needs before their own and are willing to arrange their lifestyles to accommodate the requirements of the joint custody plan.

4. Both parents have shown they can separate their role as husband or wife (where the anger started) from their role as parent.

5. Both parents have shown a reasonable ability and willingness to communicate and cooperate in matters involving the child.

6. Both parents have shown the potential to make changes in the joint custody arrangement as the developmental needs of their child change.

7. The child has special needs that require both parents to advocate on his/her behalf (For example, the child is learning-disabled, has attention deficit disorder, is developmentally delayed, or is physically challenged.)

8. The extended families of both parents, including the child's grandparents, are involved in the child's everyday life. All are cooperative with each other.

Joint custody doesn't mean a 50-50 split of the child's time. As the architect in rebuilding the family, the judge tries to design a plan that will work throughout the childhood of the child, awarding joint custody when s/he decides the preponderance of information available favors it, sometimes even when neither parent seeks it. Yet, even though such an award may mean the child lives with one parent during the week throughout the school year, the fact that both parents legally share custody of the child reduces the fears of the other parent that s/he will no longer be a significant part of the child's daily life.

Although joint custody has far fewer proponents now than in the 1980s, the debate over it continues to this day. Geography continues to play a part in a joint custody award, as do the culture and values of the local community. In California, outcome studies have tended to favor joint custody; in Vermont, the state legislature has gone on record to oppose it as detrimental to the child. No matter the location, however, the judge is the best decider of how local culture and values and the needs of the child shall be reconciled. Shared custody is a good solution for some cases with legal custody to both parents, but sole physical custody to one. In Maine, the courts routinely favor this idea.

The stress on the children is reduced and in this sense, children's rights supercede parental rights.

Visitation

Recommendations in this regard are often generic: every other weekend, Wednesday, or holiday, for example. Or they may call for parents to share or alternate having the child on school vacations and the child's birthdays and for the child to celebrate Mother's Day and Father's Day with the honored parent. But do such generic recommendations work well? Is one parent likely to be shortchanged? There is no perfect visitation arrangement following a family dissolution. A comprehensive custody report by team evaluators, with extensive background on the child's needs, (and the parents' visitation wishes) is welcomed not only by the judge but also by all parties with an interest in the visitation arrangements.

In preparing such a report, it helps to focus on child developmental stages. Is the child able to see friends and participate in sports or clubs while with each parent? Frequent use of day care, especially for a young child, usually is not advisable when the other parent is available. The child's fears and anxieties are important in making visitation recommendations. For example, a young child should not usually travel over 600 miles; this may creates separation anxiety, externding into adulthood.

Where there is high conflict (unable to resolve 75% of daily issues) between parents, the number of shifts between parental households should be minimized. In such situations, having the child visit a parent on specified weekends may be the best option—and on one afternoon per week with an overnight for a school-age child.

Where the child's safety is a concern, you may need to recommend supervision of parent-child contact. If so, discuss with your teammate and the family who might objectively supervise and intervene when necessary. A relative or close friend of either parent may be objective and familiar to the child. Paid supervision by a guardian ad litem is possible in some states. When supervision of physical contact is called for, give similar consideration to the question of unlimited phone contact, or daily text messaging or e-mails which may be stressful for the child.

On the other hand, telephone calls between visits can facilitate ongoing parent-child contact. A regular schedule of calls (not daily) can help the child adjust to the new situation and keep each parent abreast of activities in the child's life. Because contact recommendations involve juggling many complex issues crucial for the child's and the family's healthy adjustment, carefully weigh the likely effects of any recommendation from as many meaningful angles as you can before deciding to make it, keeping in mind that children are surprisingly resilient and adapt to thoughtfully crafted plans. There should be some days in a week when the child receives no contact from the parent who is residing elsewhere.

Concluding, Recommending

When, you know what you should conclude and what to recommend with regard to a particular issue of your evaluation but are concerned with its real life application, enlist the judgment and expertise of your teammate and then let your report sit on a shelf for a week. "Brewing" the decision is never a mistake.

The team approach also allows the evaluators to develop each one's information base. A psychiatrist or family practitioner can be a good team member for consultation with physicians on reported medical conditions for family members (and what the impact may be on the child or adult). Some examples of consults would be "How would Marfane Syndrome impact parenting, if at all?" "How does Hodgkin's Disease affect life span, if at all?" "How much time and expertise is required to administer certain medications for chronic childhood diseases? Supplying this information to the court helps to explain recommendations found in the report. The team report is by far more credible with both an MD and a PhD member (than a solo evaluator's submission) when a child or family member suffers from a significant medical condition.

It is helpful to choose one option for custody, instead of avoiding offering a recommendation. The judge looks at the reasoning behind the opinion as another source of information for the court. One of the complaints from judges is receiving the report from an evaluator who does not make a decision.

You must state your opinion—your conclusions and recommendations—clearly, pulling together relevant information in a way that is reasonable and makes sense in terms of the Best Interests of the Child. As the architect of the family to be rebuilt, the judge makes the final custody and visitation decisions based on your state's statutes, case law, judicial experience, all testimony and evidence, and his/her understanding of the usefulness of the custody evaluations provided.

Juvenile family court judges say that deciding the future of children is the most difficult but also most compelling part of their job. Yet decide they must, after examining custody evaluations and listening to conflicting testimony. As the courts perhaps best objective source of family information and analysis related to the custody case before it, you and your teammate have a responsibility to render an informed opinion and to make recommendations based on your expertise and judgment. You are the eyes and ears of the court and as a team the best equipped to offer some helpful, healing strategies.

Many judges have revealed during their own continuing education training, "I don't care about the evaluators' opinions as much as I care about how they came to these opinions." The team format is powerful, for it is two professionals using an established, intricate protocol to help define what is best for the children and, therefore, their families.

Chapter 4
Writing, Presenting, Defending the Report

Report Structure

Although the format for custody evaluation reports varies widely among evaluators, you and your teammate will find the outline in Table 4.1 an effective, logical way to organize your report. Basic information is listed first, followed by your opinion as evaluators, framed in terms of the Best Interests of the Child criteria for your state or as set forth in this text (see Table 1.1), with your assessment of the relevant individuals. Profiles and assessment data for each family member then follow, ending with a summary of the report and specific recommendations for visitation. Placing your opinion at the beginning of the report forces you to justify that opinion in the rest of your report. Logically laying out the information, observations, and reasoning behind it allows readers, in particular, the judge and lawyers, to follow your report more easily and to make better use of it. With the opinion at the end, readers can get lost in the data and procedures while trying to guess the outcome. I have read many evaluator reports with unexpected endings. Over working in isolation can lead to such a situation. It is especially important for the judge, who will ultimately decide the custody dispute, to understand how and why you came to your opinion so that s/he can fit your information and observations to the legal decision parameters.

The judge, the lawyers, and all adult parties to the dispute will hopefully benefit from a clear, coherent, comprehensive report based on the important information that you have gathered and observations the team has made. Indeed, preparing and writing a strong, effective report will help you present strong, effective testimony in court. Usually the senior member of the team organizes the report, incorporating the second team member's report. The recommendations are joint decisions from both team members. Separate decisions and separate reports are not complications of a team format, but rather add to the depth of thought.

Table 4.1

Generic Format for Report Organization

Basic Information

- Title of evaluation: "Family Forensic Team Custody Evaluation"
- Names of evaluation participants with dates of birth, docket number
- Names of evaluators and titles
- Date family referred
- Referral source
- Dates seen
- Hours seen
- Date report completed
- Date report mailed

Opinion (framed in terms of salient criteria, "Best Interests of the Child")

- All documents reviewed
- Historical background, couple history, or both
- Assessment procedures for each person

Document, Data, and Procedures

- Data and results from procedures synthesized in the opinion
- Profiles (behavioral, social, emotional, and developmental) formulated on
  each family member, including observations during the assessment
- Criteria considered for detection of any controversial allegations, such as sexual abuse or family violence.

Conclusion
- Report summary
- Specific visitation suggestions

What Judges Want and Need to Know

The judge sees your custody team report when it is admitted into evidence. When asked to testify by the court or one of the lawyers, request a subpoena and payment *before* you appear. Remember, no matter who pays you, your opinion can't be purchased, just your time. When testifying, be clear, concise, and candid. It is better to say, "I don't know," when you don't. Your credibility is always on the line and will be challenged if you venture beyond your level of expertise (see the guidelines under "Testifying" below).

An evaluator's professional opinions are based on the type of information typically used for making clinical assessments and treatment decisions. A judge, in turn, makes a legal custody ruling based, at least in part, on the expert testimony of one or more evaluators. Judges may issue findings of fact, which explain their reasoning and rulings and provide the basis for appeals, although, in some states, they are not required to do so.

Listed below are eighteen questions typically raised by judges in complex custody disputes, often in cases where abuse or neglect has been alleged or documented.

1. What are the child's present and future developmental needs?

2. Can the parents reasonably meet the child's developmental needs? If so, how? If not, what other resources are available?

3. What is the child's emotional relationship to each parent and to siblings or other persons in the home?

4. Do the parents have empathy for the child, other adults, and themselves?

5. How does the child's family pattern compare to typically chaotic, dysfunctional, neglectful families?

6. What is the behavioral and psychological profile of each of the parents? Does it fit the profile of an abusive or neglectful parent?

7. How does the child's present development compare to that of normal children? How did parenting, poverty, the environment, abuse, neglect, and other factors contribute to the child's profile?

8. Does the child exhibit any particular syndrome, such as Failure to Thrive, Fetal Alcohol Syndrome, Reactive Attachment Disorder, Pervasive Developmental Disorder, or Attention Deficit Disorder (ADD) that needs to be described and acted upon?

9. If the parents are in need of rehabilitation, what resources are available to them? How long should such rehabilitation take, and under what conditions?

10. If in temporary custody, how long might the child remain there before his/her development is adversely affected? Would returning the child to one or both of his/her parents be more detrimental than leaving the child in temporary custody or putting the child in another permanent home?

11. At what point is the child unable to be reached through outpatient treatment? Would residential treatment be warranted?

12. What are reasonable dispositional alternatives, and should supervised visitation be encouraged? Under what circumstances?

13. If either parent is undergoing drug treatment, how can the court determine when that treatment has been sufficient for the child to be returned home safely? For how long must drug abuse have ceased in the home? What are the consequences of neglect from drug abuse?

14. Can children be placed in a home where neglect or abuse has been denied repeatedly?

15. Does the child or the child's family have special issues not addressed in the custody evaluation? If so, what are they and do they require additional evaluation? Should there be another evaluation in a year?

16. Should the court review this family's postdivorce adjustment? If so, at what intervals and for how long? Are six-month reviews too often?

17. Is the child's family psychologically healthy? In what specific senses?

18. Can the problems experienced by the child's family or the child be reasonably attributed to normal postdivorce adjustment?

Pulling It All Together

To produce an excellent report, you and your teammate must pull together and synthesize a large amount of information in nontechnical language. The better you do this, the stronger your report and testimony will be. The following steps can facilitate the process.

1. Prepare to write your report by maintaining a well-organized case file from the outset of your

evaluation. Arrange your information in the order you collect it, carefully numbering each page, separating your handwritten notes and work product from testing materials and questionnaires, and grouping the information by family member. Organize all notes and test results and submitted lawyer-client information in a format that can be easily cross-referenced a year or two later.

2. Keep in mind the Best Interests of the Child criteria as defined by your state or set forth in this text (see table 1.1) at each step of your evaluation and as you set about writing your report.

3. Request, obtain and review all relevant, available health or medical and school records, sometimes on both child and parent, personal histories, previous evaluations, assessments, and any other significant references for the most complete background on all family members involved that time and resources permit.

4. Describe what a psychologically healthy family, child, and adult are in your report. Doing so not only provides crucial reference points but also serves to educate the parties involved, showing judge and lawyers alike what you know and what they must know to understand your evaluation.

5. Prepare a profile of each child in careful detail. Children cannot speak for themselves and have a limited ability to show who they are and what they need. This is your chance to speak for them. Working together, you and your teammate can do this efficiently even for large families.

6. Explain the quality of the relationship between each child and each parent, stepparent, grandparent, sibling, and other significant person

in that child's everyday life. This is a key factor for the judge's decision making. You both can do this best when both interview all significant persons and compare your appraisals. Each team member must have his or her own opinion in this area.

7. Note the strengths and weaknesses of each parent, regardless of who you recommend for custody. This provides your evaluation with balance, respect, thoroughness, and perspective, as well as empathy for the human condition of both parents. Since each of you interviews them several times, you and your teammate can avoid favoring one parent over the other by having spent more time with a parent as needed.

8. Keep an open mind as you review the information you have gathered. Watch for biases, myths, and assumptions you or your teammate may hold, as well as the effects of outside pressure or concern about potential repercussions—and correct for them with team feedback.

9. Based on your and your teammate's review and discussion of the information gathered and the developmental needs of each child, form a clear, final opinion. Don't waffle. (If you need more information, obtain it, and so, too, the waffling stops).

10. Create a first draft, using a generic organization format such as shown in Table 4.1 that allows for a full explanation and justification of your opinion backed by gathered information and based on Best Interests of the Child criteria. Take turns with your teammate playing devil's advocate. Be prepared to respond—with information—to questions, challenges, and even skepticism from the judge, the lawyers, or both.

11. Let the draft sit for a week and then reread it. This will increase your chances of spotting overlooked details about family issues and areas where more information may be needed. "Brew" the decisions.

12. Set yourself a reasonable deadline, and fill in any gaps in the materials you have assembled. If you do not, the lawyers will almost certainly point out the missing information.

13. Refine your first draft, writing as much as you need to make your points clearly and effectively—but no more. Your and your teammate's combined reports should run between 15 and 30 pages, depending on the number of family members evaluated and the complexity of the family issues surrounding the custody dispute.

14. For best results and to minimize the anxiety of the waiting family, issue your report within 30 days of your final interviews. A child's sense of time is based on his/her age, not on your sense of time. Children deserve timely answers to their future living arrangements.

15. The report should be sent only to the court or attorneys, not to the parents. It contains information that should not be distributed to non-officers of the court. Explain this to the parents at the initial meeting with them. You cannot stop attorneys from distributing your team report, but you can put a disclaimer on the top of it (not to be distributed to non-officers of the court).

Expert Testimony: Presenting and Defending Your Report

Once qualified as expert witnesses, you and your evaluator teammate have an obligation to the court to provide information collected during your evaluation and an expert opinion based on that information within the constraints imposed by your discipline's code of ethics. This requires that you know the guidelines for forensic testimony and that you have knowledge beyond the case at hand from the fields of child and adult development, psychopathology, child forensic issues, and couple and family systems. The expert witness uses literature in the fields of forensic and general psychology, psychiatry, and sociology to support as well as to explain an opinion. For custody evaluators, the scope of expertise includes at least twelve areas forming a specialized body of knowledge useful to the court:

1. The Best Interests of the Child criteria (including the developmental needs of the child) as defined by state statute or case law or as set forth in the Best Interests blueprint of this text.

2. Child and adult development theory and current as well as classic publications and research on children, divorce, and specific decision outcomes for issues such as visitation and shared custody.

3. Research and theory on children's reactions to trauma and loss.

4. Present developmental (emotional, social, physical, behavioral, educational) and special needs of each child.

5. Social history of each child, the couple, and each adult member of the family.

6. Standardized personality or child assessment profiles for all family members involved; *Diagnostic and Statistical Manual of Mental Disorders* (DSM-IV-TR) diagnoses; whether psychological or psychiatric disorders are present or absent in any adult or child evaluated; the nature of such disorders, prognosis; and treatment alternatives.

7. Children's behavioral and emotional profiles representative of present or past trauma.

8. Basic medical, psychological, social, and school background information on all family members involved, based on review of official records, including day care records; therapists' treatment summaries; and so on.

9. Present behavioral and emotional profile of each child in school, home, community, with peers, and during visitation.

10. History of each child's past and present emotional attachments and physical time with parental figures, siblings, child care providers, grandparents, friends, governess or nanny, and so on.

11. Common parental fitness criteria and each parent's capacity to demonstrate them, including knowledge of child development, ability to demonstrate empathy and affection, discipline techniques, role boundaries, education, values, and history of parenting.

12. Quality of parental care, nurturance, and guidance of each child and of parental attention to that child's medical, social, and educational needs.

The psychologist, psychiatrist, social worker, court-connected evaluator, as an expert witness must be thoroughly familiar with his/her particular discipline's body of knowledge and the ethical, educational, and research guidelines for expert testimony. What the judge learns is based on what you are asked and answer, not on what you want to say. Your report will also speak for you, when it is admitted into evidence. Understanding what a judge needs to know to make a decision helps to make your report and your testimony as an expert witness focused, cogent, and useful.

In testifying about information you have gathered in the light of your specialized training, it's best to speak in plain English, as objectively as you can, keeping psychological jargon or diagnostic terminology to a minimum, especially when describing behavior. Basing their decisions on the Best Interests of the Child, judges must make their rulings and findings of fact free of clinical psychological jargon.

To qualify as expert witnesses, you (and at times, your evaluator teammate) must be prepared to demonstrate your knowledge in relevant areas. You should be prepared to describe your training and work experience, memberships in professional organizations, publications in your field, journals you read, your teaching and research. You should also be prepared to describe generic protocols used in custody evaluations by you, your team, and other evaluators. Usually, the team member who organizes the evaluation and interacts with the referring court or lawyers, is the one who goes to court as needed and testifies for the team.

TESTIFYING

The following guidelines will serve you and your teammate well when you are called upon to testify in court.

- Understand what you will experience: the subpoena service; the deposition; the voir dire; the direct examination, the cross examination; the redirect and the re-cross examination. The theatre of the courthouse.

- Prepare in advance for any of the above. Understand the legal basis for your work in and out of court. Ask to be enlightened about the lawyers' strategies with you as the expert.

- Be certain that you not only have an evaluator team pretrial conference, but that you also know what is in team files and that they are in order.

- Prepare with your teammate for the expected challenges to your opinion and your work.

- Rehearse your findings for each Best Interests criteria (10) and how (you and your teammate) arrived at these opinions.

- Read several good treatises on the expert in child custody battles and seek advice on courtroom conduct. Watch some expert testimony if you are a novice.

- Be current on pertinent research, publications and test construction.

- Carefully review and plan your testimony beforehand. Be thoroughly familiar with everything you wrote in your report. This will let you testify with confidence, clarity, and precision.

- Look directly at the judge when you testify, not at the lawyers or courtroom personnel.

- Answer questions with a simple yes or no—or straight to the point. Elaborate only when asked to do so, and only as much as you need to.

- When testifying, be conscious of how you react to stress. If you sense you're becoming defensive, argumentative, or arrogant, self-correct as often as you need to. Watch seasoned forensic experts testify. Note how they respond and how they deal with stress. Use techniques of relaxation response, such as regulated breathing (don't forget to exhale) or tightening and relaxing your hand or foot muscles, to manage your stress—especially when being cross-examined. Remember, cross-examination is a legal action by an advocate for one of the parties, usually not a personal attack, no matter how aggressive the advocate may seem. If your mouth or throat becomes dry but your hand is shaking from stress, use a mint instead of drinking water.

- Keep cool. Don't be intimidated by a lawyer who stands too close or scoffs at your statements. Look to the judge as you answer.

- If you don't understand a question, ask for clarification or to have the question repeated. You are responsible for taking care of yourself; the lawyers and judge will not. And you are the expert on the ethical standards for your particular discipline. When, for example, they require you to reveal test items abide by the acceptable standards, no matter what the court may order.

- When a question goes beyond your expertise, it's best to say you don't know or can't answer that question. Keep in mind your discipline's latest ethical guidelines and be prepared to recite them.

- Report only information you are sure of, especially from research or studies, do not embellish fact or answer more than necessary.

- When asked to testify on your assessments, evaluations, or concluding opinion, remember your job is to provide information, not manipulate it.

- When asked to testify on child sexual abuse, report only evidence you have obtained or observed, you are not the trier of fact, nor do you render an opinion on credibility of a client. For example, you might report that the child has a profile commonly seen in child sexual abuse victims and state what the child has reported to you, but not state the child was abused.

- Stay quiet while in or around court; keep to yourself even at lunch. Avoid talking to the attorneys or addressing the judge unless you are addressed by them. Stay neutral.

- Keep in mind that the outcome of the custody dispute is up to the judge —*not* to you.

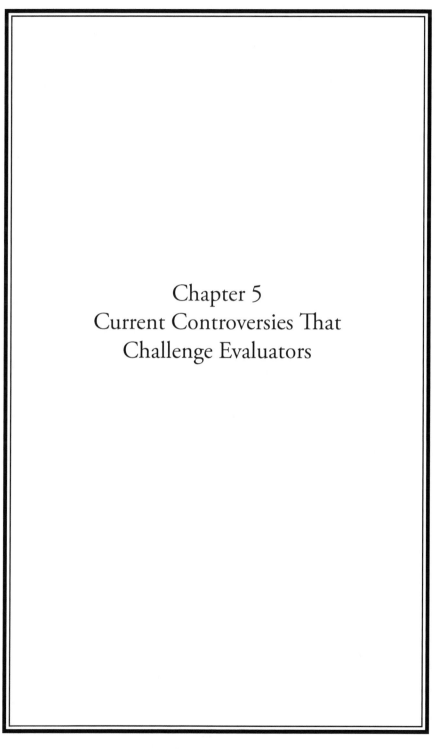

Chapter 5
Current Controversies That
Challenge Evaluators

This chapter will highlight some of the controversial issues in the field of child custody evaluations. If your evaluation involves one or more of these issues, I can't recommend strongly enough that you read the relevant current literature for greater depth. A complex referral, involving child sexual abuse allegations embedded in a child custody evaluation, is simply best investigated by a forensic team along with social services and each state's legal professionals. Issues addressed in this chapter also require in depth investigative interviewing to determine the best placement for the children. Judges look to evaluators to provide needed background information and analysis in deciding what to do when such issues are put before them in custody cases. Expert testimony and reports, as well as community culture and beliefs, sometimes combine to produce varying outcomes on the following issues that custody evaluators must consider:

- Incest or sexual abuse allegations in a divorcing couple;
- Placing siblings in separate homes;
- Prolonged disputes over a child's primary home;
- Alienation of a child from one parent;
- Equally unfit parents;
- Allegations of domestic violence;
- Long-distance moves planned by the parent with temporary custody;
- Gay or Lesbian or Transgender parenting;
- Grandparent visitation rights denied by one of the parents.

Incest and Sexual Abuse Allegations

When you encounter unexpected and new incest or sexual abuse allegations in the course of your evaluation, you'll need to immediately report them to your appropriate state agency, such as the Department of Health and Human Services; then, report these to the court and request permission to validate them before making your final recommendations on custody and visitation. You may wait for a validation to be done. To perform such validations, you must be trained in and strictly follow specific procedures, which vary from jurisdiction to jurisdiction. Some counties in New York State, for example, require that the validation interview with the child be videotaped and performed by only a court appointed validater. Where videotaping is not required, make sure you know what is expected and should you audiotape the alleged victim's interview, have it transcribed verbatim. This knowledge can prevent problems later when testifying in court about what procedures you used with the child/victim and what questions you asked. It also promotes justice for the child and family. Unfortunately, unfounded abuse allegations can be effective in a temporary custody award to one of the parents.

Considerable literature has articulated the lasting effects of sexual abuse on children. Table 5.1 summarizes a myriad of symptoms associated with child sexual abuse. Keep in mine, each victim is uniquely wounded and careful examination of the issues and the child involves a special protocol for the interview and review of all data pertaining to the allegation. No list of symptoms is a determinant of abuse. Many symptoms are not confined to certain ages or stages. Child Forensic evaluators are highly skilled in the field of sexual abuse validations. A child abuse evaluation is a specialty area of forensic psychologists and psychiatrists. However, make certain that during the course of the custody evaluation this is a new report and then contact Child Protective Services. If it is not a new report, the senior team evaluator requests background.

Table 5.1
**Developmental Stage[1]* – Related Symptoms Commonly Reported
For Victims of Sexual Abuse in the Literature**

Stage(s): Age	Symptoms
Infancy, Early Childhood: Birth – to 4 years to 6 years of age	• Fearfulness • Clinging behavior • Developmental delays • Suspicious physical findings (hymenal tear, etc.) • Staring blankly • Mood swings • Whining • Withdrawing • Daydreaming • Sexual play with dolls • Compulsive masturbation • Elevated blood pressure • Psychosomatic problems (rash, pain in leg, etc.) • Inability to learn • Insomnia • Crying out in sleep • Fear of certain types of people • School problems • Sudden onset of anxiety • Depression
Middle and Late Childhood: 6 – 11 years	• Insomnia • Self Mutilation • Overeating • School failure • Truancy • Running away • Sudden irritability • Excessive bathing • Psychosomatic problems • Suspicious physical findings • Staring blankly • Cruelty to others, animals • Mood swings • Withdrawing • Lying • Cheating • Secretiveness • Daydreaming

---

* Some victims show varying or no signs or symptoms as listed, chronologically, in this table. Not evidence based.

Stage(s): Age	Symptoms
Middle and Late Childhood: 6 – 11 years Cont'd	• Sexual play, preoccupation • Seductive behavior • Low self esteem • Compulsive masturbation • Enuresis, Encopresis
Early Adolescence: 12– 16 years	• Depression • Guilt • Anxiety • Low self-esteem • Isolation • Poor body image/obesity • Self Mutilation • Staring blankly • Cruelty to others • Mood swings • Withdrawing • Lying • Cheating • Aggressiveness • Secretiveness • Daydreaming • Sexual preoccupation • Sexual abuse of younger children • Suicidal ideation • Depression • Truancy • Running away • Seductive behavior • Sexual identity issues • Pregnancy • School problems • Compulsive cleanliness

Late Adolescence: 16– 22years	• Self-depreciation • Prostitution or promiscuity • Depression • Isolation • Rebellion • Pregnancy • Venereal disease • Drug abuse • Eating disorders (anorexia, bulimia, compulsive eating). • Self harm/victimization (recurrent)

Stage(s): Age	Symptoms
Late Adolescence: 16 – 22 years Cont'd	<ul><li>Aggressiveness</li><li>Seductive behavior</li><li>Sexual avoidance or preoccupation</li><li>Low self-esteem</li><li>Sexual abuse of younger children</li><li>Suicidal ideation</li><li>Lying</li><li>Cheating</li><li>Mood swings</li><li>Poor body image</li><li>Sexual identity issues</li><li>School problems</li><li>Running away</li><li>Compulsive cleanliness</li></ul>
Adulthood: 21 years and up	<ul><li>Eating disorders (anorexia, bulimia)</li><li>Anxiety</li><li>Phobias</li><li>Suicide attempts</li><li>Low self-esteem</li><li>Guilt</li><li>Feelings of defenselessness</li><li>Feelings of worthlessness</li><li>Seductive behavior</li><li>Sexual avoidance or promiscuity</li><li>Abusing others</li><li>Onset of psychological or personality disorders</li><li>Drug abuse</li><li>Self-destructiveness(Self Mutilation, etc.)</li><li>Angry outbursts</li><li>Somatic problems</li><li>Childhood memory loss</li><li>Sexual maladjustment</li></ul>

Incest or Sexual Abuse Allegations: When and Why They Arise During a Custody Battle:

- A vulnerable situation
  Visitation or living alone with a poorly coping, regressive parent may leave the child vulnerable to being treated as a substitute spouse, or to being abused by those who seek vulnerable children.

- A safe environment
  The alleged offender may, at last, be out of the home because the couple separated. The threat of retaliation is removed. The child victim is safer. The child may then remember the abuse. The other parent may choose to disclose prior concerns. Sexual offenders often marry adults who have children of an appealing age. Sometimes several generations of children are abused. If the offender is highly respected in the community, the children may have kept quiet because of the "cloak of respectability" around the adult. Once divorce occurs, however, the children may disclose information.

- Revenge
  One parent becomes displaced by the other's lover, and the triangle engenders deep anger and loss. An innocent statement by the child may be exaggerated or distorted. Sexual abuse allegations are powerful weapons in child custody battles. A temporary award of custody may result from the ploy of raising abuse as an issue.

- Sensational scapegoating
  The reorganized family system, with new members and friends, may include a new, resented rival or stepparent, who is then blamed for some form of abuse.

- The inclination to notice during evaluative meetings
  A newly divorcing parent seeks support and, in the context of a family assessment, describes the child's unusual profile at school and prior sexualized behaviors.

- Programming to win
  The child has been shaped and encouraged to report abuse. Children can be influenced to report abuse that did not

occur. One paranoid parent told a nightly bedtime story about what daddy had done when the six year old child was an infant. The child then reported the abuse.

Consider the following questions if you assess incest or sexual abuse reports.

1. Does the child have many characteristics commonly seen in incest or sexual abuse victims? Is there a validation report supported by objective information as well as disclosure? Review the Child Behavior Checklist (Achenbach, 2007) and score it, comparing each parent's report of the child's profile to the school's if possible. Is there a discrepancy that is unexplained?

2. Does or did the family have a profile commonly seen in incestuous or sexually dysfunctional families? Refer to reference texts in the field commonly cited as authoritative. Was either parent a child victim themselves? Does either live with a known sex offender?

3. Does the alleged offender have a profile commonly seen in pedophiles or incest offenders? Know the literature currently being cited. The court decides guilt, not you.

4. Does the child's behavioral profile fit what the parent, school, and pediatrician report? Spend time observing the child and collecting reports from many sources. Report the results in detail.

5. Are a parent's grounds for accusing the other of sexual abuse in the home realistic or unrealistic? Does the accusing parent show signs of confabulation of having a histrionic-antisocial or borderline personality disorder, or of being an overly intrusive or highly domineering and manipulative parent? Discuss these profiles from questions 1 to 5 with your teammate.

6. Do the child's drawings of his/her worst memories include sexual victimization? Does the child draw pictures of violent events but deny s/he has experienced any violence?

7. Why is the child or parent now disclosing abuse? Are there reasons for the child or parent to do so falsely? Why *now*?

8. Has either parent had a history of abusing or being abused? Are there parallels to the parent's and child's past abuse/chaos/attachment problems?

9. Did another family member or friends know of the abuse at the time it happened? When did it happen, in terms of the post–separation or –divorce timeline? Pay especial attention to sibling reports. Siblings often know each other's secrets.

10. Does one parent seem upset and the other indifferent to the child's report of abuse? *Why?*

11. Does your teammate find the abuse allegation to have merit or to be suspicious in its timing? *Why?*

12. Does a counselor who has worked with the child confirm reports of the alleged abuse? *Why or why not?*

Placing Siblings in Separate Homes

Placing siblings together in the same home allows them to support each other as they adjust to the divorce and to have a similar social history and shared memories of family life as adults. Indeed, most custody decisions, whether they award sole custody to one parent or joint custody to both, place the children together in the home of one parent. A sibling is a good ally in later life when facing the challenges of adulthood.

On occasion, however, custody of siblings is "split" between the parents, with one or more children being placed in the home of each parent. In most cases, a parent has visitation rights for the children not in his/her care, with the two groups often brought together each weekend. Split custody is usually awarded because the older children have expressed their preference for it, because one child is tormenting another, or because the children have different fathers or mothers, provided the parents live near one another and each parent has shown a reasonable ability both to respect each other and to foster continuing relations between separated siblings.

Recommendations for split custody should be made cautiously; separation of siblings can have significant, long-term negative effects on sibling relations, particularly where there is a high level of conflict between parents. Does the children's stated preference for split custody stem from the dynamics of the parents' conflict, where, each siding with a parent, they are acting out the conflict between themselves? Do the reasons the children give for their preference (educational needs or opportunities, peer relations) have merit and would they be better served by split custody, provided of course both parents seem up to such an arrangement? Among the most significant issues in considering separation of siblings is the safety of a child. Is a sibling being repeatedly physically aggressive, emotionally or sexually abusive toward that child? In such cases, split custody may be the recommendation.

Prolonged Disputes

When one or both parents do not or cannot take the child's perspective and want to win no matter what, when parents continuously show violent disrespect for each other and or when one or both suffer from a personality or mood disorder or from just being "strange," the custody dispute and the child's distress are likely to be prolonged.

In such cases, the child is slow to recover from the pain and stress brought about by the pre-divorce, and parts of the child's development—social, behavioral, emotional, educational, and personal—is usually impacted. It falls to the evaluators to address the child's developmental needs (sense of permanence, safety, etc.) and to make specific recommendations to help bring the custody dispute to an end. Recommending a workable but specific visitation schedule may also help keep the focus on the child's needs as this is happening. In extreme cases, lasting 3–10 years, the custody dispute ends only when one parent is granted full control of the child, with the other being denied visitation. Although, paradoxically, sometimes the parent who loves the child more than him/herself gives in and lets go, attempting to 'save' the child from further harm. Because the loss of a parent at an early age has a profound impact for life, to give some relief to the child in prolonged disputes, the judge may have ordered that parents each spend blocks of time with the child or that they enter into mediation to resolve their chronic dispute. Children need—and deserve—a speedy resolution from constant uncertainty. In a tiny minority of cases (perhaps no more than 3 percent), however, this is simply not the outcome.

Alienation of Child from One Parent

This usually occurs when a parent creates an untenable situation so the child feels s/he has to choose between the parents. In this way, a parent's hostility for the other parent is transferred to the child and the child is alienated from or distrustful of the disparaged parent. This can be accomplished by making up stories, such as "Your father sexually abused you, but you can't remember so I don't want you to go." Or the hostile parent may tell other adults stories with the child present, such as "When Janie goes out, her mom shows sex movies." The hostile parent's anger at the other parent makes the child too anxious to visit him/her and impairs the child's adjustment to the new visitation arrangements. For example, the hostile parent may say, "Your father has a new girlfriend who is mean, so you shouldn't go," or "Your mom was mean to you and here's what she did when you were little." The younger the child, the easier it is for a hostile parent to cause parental alienation. Children subjected to such behavior may show signs of stress, illogical favoritism, or "battle fatigue."

The ways a hostile parent can alienate the child from the other parent need not be so obvious. If, for example, an adolescent child says, "I'm not going over to Mom's because she doesn't take me places," a hostile father can encourage the child not to visit his mother simply by saying, "Okay, you don't have to go." Or if the other parent has enrolled the child in an activity such as sports or Scouts, the hostile parent can simply not take the child to the activity when the child is with him/her.

Extended family members can also alienate the child from a parent. For example, a hostile paternal grandmother may say: "Your mother has lots of boyfriends; it's not safe for you there," or "Where did you get those awful clothes? I can't believe your mother doesn't spend money on you after all your dad gives her." Similarly, a hostile parent's comments about the other parent's new partner can achieve the same result—alienating the child from the other parent. For example, speaking of the child's stepmother, a hostile mother may say, "Don't let her take you to a doctor's appointment. Only your father or I can do that." Or, speaking of the child's stepfather, a hostile father may say, "Remember, he's *not* your father. Don't call him 'Daddy.'"

When assessing such alienating behavior, you should look for personality problems in the parents or grandparents. You may find paranoia, antisocial traits, or dependent and borderline personality disorders in such cases. On the other hand, many parents or grandparents who engage in alienating behavior are simply angry, and have let their anger go too far.

Equally Unfit Parents

Evaluating "his and her nannies" as caretakers because each parent is "very busy" and may not be at home for weeks at a time is a painful experience. But such cases are by no means rare. You may have to conclude that both parents are "equally unfit" when, after careful assessment, you and your teammate find that neither has the capacity to meet the child's needs at a minimally acceptable level. Both parents may display strong antisocial attitudes, or be engaged in illegal or drug-related activity. They may hold extreme beliefs that interfere with raising a child, for example, that showing pornography or giving alcohol or drugs to young children is okay. Or they may not believe in ever consulting a doctor no matter what the medical problem. Both parents may be unpredictable or lead highly indulgent lives, frequently changing residences or relationships. One may have an uncontrollable temper; the other, uncontrollable companions. Lacking any genuine interest in parenting, they may fight over who has to take the child. In such cases, you may have to "rule out" both parents as fit and to recommend placing their children with a third party. This may be a relative, such as a grandparent, or a foster parent. Wherever possible, you and your teammate should evaluate the other party, and if more than one person is available, offer the court your recommendation about rehabilitation of at least one parent.

A Couple With Some Allegations of Domestic Violence

Always keep the adults scheduled on separate dates and follow any court orders that exist. Children who witness domestic violence are victims, too and have a helpless sense of responsibility; they need a way out. A batterer spouse will likely batter his/her new partner or spouse, and a battered spouse untreated will likely take up with or choose another abusive mate. That being the case, you need to examine more than the physical and emotional abuse in the child's household. Which parent, if any, has sought help for him/herself? For the children? Which parent denies what's been going on and blames the other? Which has taken the time and trouble to address his/her behavior?

Although many parents who are involved in domestic violence either witnessed or were themselves victims of such violence as children, some will not recall such childhoods. Denial will be strong. "Were you abused as a child?" Parent: "Not that I recall". Be certain you are knowledgeable about the profile of offenders who are most likely to be able to change. Married with a job and a high school education are hopeful predictors of change after anger management group training.

Long-Distance Moves Planned by the Parent with Temporary Custody

Is a long-distance move a means of gaining full control of the child or getting even for an unwanted divorce? Why is this planned? Are there good reasons to do this now?

When one parent moves far away from the other, this can greatly impede the child's visitation with the other parent, grandparents, or both, whether by design or happenstance. Should a six-year-old daughter, relocated with her custodial mother to Honolulu, Hawaii, be asked to fly from there to Tuscaloosa, Alabama, to see her father? Is the transfer of her mother's new spouse to Honolulu a compelling reason to end the father's access? Should she lose access to her father? Or should the court now award custody of the child to the father if he is equally fit so that she can remain in her childhood community? If so, should the child now lose access to her mother? Does either arrangement mean visitation with the non-custodial parent must become infrequent, or should the parents now be required to travel more to ensure that won't be the case?

Custody evaluators are inclined to recommend, and judges to rule, that the child remain within his/her hometown surroundings and available to grandparents and other caring people in the community. But this may not always be the wisest course to take. As with other issues discussed above, focusing on the Best Interests of the Child, you and your teammate must consider the painful consequences of a long-distance move by a parent who may have many reasons for such a plan.

Gay, Lesbian or Transgender Parenting

Should custody of a daughter or son be awarded to a lesbian mother or gay father? Should sexual orientation of a parent matter? Does dad becoming a female cause too much stress for a child? The answer depends in large part on the locale (San Francisco or Salt Lake City, for example). The judge knows the local community's values, culture, biases, and standards for what is acceptable in that community and under state law. If in the custody of a gay, lesbian, or transgender parent, a report must indicate what are the likely effects of living with that parent, both positive and negative, on the child's development? These are some of the questions you and your evaluator teammate must address before making your recommendations. One teenager said, "I'm just used to it; it's no big deal." Another, younger child was unhappy about the "coming out" of a gay parent and wanted to live with the heterosexual parent. The outcome of each case must be based on the Best Interests of the Child, not on the sexual orientation of the parent. But such cases may make family court judges uneasy, no matter what the final determination. One team member needs to clearly address this issue with all involved.

Grandparent Visitation Rights

Although grandparent visitation law is not relatively new, there is little literature on the subject. All fifty states have adopted statutes in this regard and based them on Best Interests of the Child criteria. As you and your teammate address this issue, consider the following factors: the child's adjustment to home, school, and community; the past and present relationship of the child to each grandparent in the child's life and that of each grandparent to the child's parents; the mental and physical health of each grandparent; the ability and disposition of each grandparent to contribute to the child's developmental needs, to communicate and cooperate with the custodial parent or parents, and to meet the child's special needs. Many grandparents help children weather the storms of divorce by providing reassurance and relief. Although many are a source of unconditional love for a child and of support for the child's positive development, some are not. To determine whether their role in the child's life is beneficial and will likely remain so, fully evaluate both grandparents using the evaluation procedures for parents described above. Assess their motivation for requesting visitation at this particular time. Interview each grandparent alone with each child and as a couple with all the children in a group. Have the grandparents demonstrated affection, empathy, and consistency in their relations with each child? What is their knowledge of child development? What are their role expectations? Their attitudes toward child rearing? Pay especial attention to the grandparents' relationship with the child's parents. For example, if the mother's parents are litigating for increased visitation, whether she is the custodial parent or not, are there problems between them? This should be explored and discussed. Old, unresolved issues may be fueling battles over visitation, as may previous custody proceedings. Has there recently been, for example, a bitter custody dispute that the mother "lost"? Or is there a motion to modify custody now pending? If a father accused and convicted of sexual abuse is denied custody by the court, what happens to his mother's and father's visitation rights?

As in intact families, so in a divorcing family, the needs of the child to maintain and foster relations with his/her parents should supersede the needs of the grandparents to have access. Grandparent access that significantly interferes with the child's adjustment at home, at school, or in the community doesn't serve the Best Interests of the Child. Moreover, even in the best of situations, grandparents are biased toward one of the child's parents (and not always their own adult child). Whether the grandparents can play a beneficial role in the child's life depends on the extent to which they have had a balanced relationship with both of the child's parents before the separation; the maturity and mental health of each grandparent; the status of their marriages; and their attitudes about children.

Other questions to consider include: How long was the child involved with the grandparents before visitation stopped? How regular were their visits? What role did the grandparents play in contributing to the child's normal development? What role do they intend to play, now and in the future? Do the grandparents understand the child's needs, and are they willing and able to put them ahead of their own? One still grieving grandmother insisted the six year old grandchild, on every visit, go to the cemetery to visit her deceased mother. Unwilling to listen to the child's upset, the grandmother lost visitation rights, unless supervised.

When the child's father or mother does not have visitation rights, you should consider the question of visitation for the father's or mother's parents very carefully. The child may experience considerable stress during such visitation, seeing in the visiting grandparent the parent who is not visiting. When sexual abuse allegations have been made, give particular consideration to the grandparents' attitude toward them. When unsupervised, grandparent visitation has been denied by the court. You may consider recommending that telephone contact, e-mail, and text messaging not be allowed either.

Concluding Thoughts

Guided by the polestar of the child-centered, parent-sensitive Best Interests of the Child, evaluators, through team information gathering, analysis, and recommendations, and judges, through findings of fact and rulings, do their best to help families torn apart by divorce. Increasingly, over the last two decades or so, lawyers have come to represent a child's Best Interests as the child's attorney or court-appointed special advocate (guardian *ad litem*). Following a strict code of ethics and custody report guidelines for child custody evaluations, forensic evaluators have increasingly come to strive to combine objectivity and excellence. But we must always remember there are no "right" answers to custody issues that won't be questioned tomorrow. The developmental needs of the child and childhood wait for no court calendar. We work carefully to keep an eye on the future with team assessments promoting an in depth look with special blueprints for Rebuilding Families that present unusual challenges to the custody evaluators and the court.

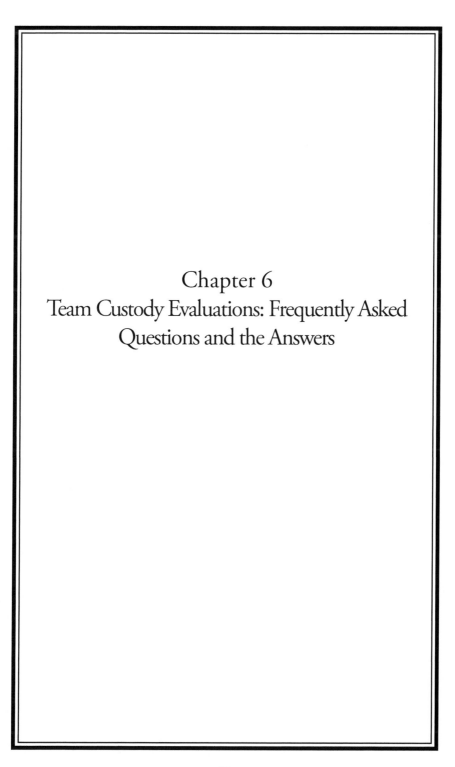

Chapter 6
Team Custody Evaluations: Frequently Asked
Questions and the Answers

The team custody evaluation relies not only on a ten point 'Blueprint,' the Polestar 'Best Interests of the Child' but also has within the multiple days of assessment the "Family Living Laboratory." This unique protocol is clear in offering an opportunity for the child(ren) to share their emotional world with evaluators, who observe family dynamics, and adult world views and personalities. The needs, current and future of the child(ren) and family are appreciated and respected as they unfold within this evaluation.

The team approach, offering fresh information and extra time for explanations and inquiry, now should be considered a real alternative to a solo expert's decision making approach with only testing as a teammate.

Common questions and answers about how to proceed have come from many of my students including family court judges, child forensic evaluators, psychologists, psychology interns, child psychiatrists, medical residents, social workers, social work students and other court personnel.

Here are some answers to important questions:

Question: Who writes the report to the court?

Answer: The lead evaluator writes the team opinion and both evaluators write separate reports that are part of the opinion.

Question: Must the protocol be used only with a multidisciplinary team?

Answer: No, two psychologists with complimentary expertise do very well with this protocol. One member of the team should always be a psychologist because of the skill levels in both assessment and interviewing.

Question: Why use a multidisciplinary team?

Answer   The family often comes in with both complex psychological and medical or social histories. The team that is best equipped for any issues is the psychologist-psychiatrist model with one of them being a child specialist. An astute chairman of a College of Medicine's Family Practice department has worked with me as have talented court social workers and astute child psychiatrists. The team reports were enriched by their insights and observations.

Question: Won't this approach cost too much for most families?

Answer: Child custody evaluations are not covered by health insurance and are expensive, whether using a solo or team format. However, the efficiency and structure of the team protocol rarely costs more, if at all. The expense is a set fee paid two weeks before the evaluation is scheduled to begin.

Question: Would the team leader, with more to do, be paid more?

Answer: Yes and the leader may be a full time Forensic Specialist, whereas a teammate may do court related work only part-time.

Question: How can you issue a team report within 30 days of the last face to face meeting? Most evaluators do not.

Answer: Deadlines are made clear at the start of the evaluation. The parents are asked to bring specific background information with them; the attorneys' letters arrive one week prior to the evaluation of the clients. The parents' final written statements must arrive within seven days after leaving the team evaluation. The smart team stays on target with each member working on agreed tasks.

A stale mass of information does a disservice to the court, the clients and especially the consideration of the child's best interest. Sharing the workload is most helpful for busy clinicians.

Question: What does go wrong with this format?

Answer: Unreliability and the weather are the two main foes in my practice history. Some team evaluators (such as a taxed psychiatry resident or psychology post doctorate intern) may miss deadlines to produce a report.

Some parents show up late in the morning and therefore stay later. Sometimes the evaluation must have a third day added due to illness or snow storms, or abuse allegations.

Question: Who testifies in court?

Answer: The team member who is subpoened (one or both) testifies. Sometimes testimony is without subpoena and only the team leader testifies. The psychologist, of course, must testify to any test batteries.

Question: Do team members disagree on the team's opinion?

Answer: Rarely. The team discusses the data after thinking about it for a week. Shelving a draft of a report is very helpful as is respect for the teammate's work. Good minds with enough objective information (that is key) tend to agree. Team conferences are enlightening. There are usually three or four. Since members issue their own part of the team report, separate opinions have a place to be noted.

Question: What is the one main advantage of teamwork versus the solo evaluator's work?

Answer: Primarily teams offer an in depth, understandable comprehensive opportunity to all clients to be understood and heard. The unexpected can be accommodated and the expected is expanded upon. Two heads are better than one. A secondary result is that whether clients like the outcome or not, few file formal complaints because two professionals, as a team, with a clear protocol, worked together and engaged the family in rebuilding.

Question: Is there a guideline for ethical behavior for team custody evaluations?

Answer: The only specific mention of this issue is from the Association of Family and Conciliation Courts (AFCC) in a May, 2006, reissue of ethical guidelines. It states briefly that "Any evaluator who does this team work must be qualified in their own right, to perform such works and be answerable for the forensic work product." I have seen no other guidelines, but ethical guidelines (for solo evaluators) prevail based on the discipline's requirements

Question: Does the team schedule a third day for some clients?

Answer: Yes. Illness of a client during the evaluation or unexpected new events might be causes for this. There is a decision by the team within two weeks of the first meeting when another day is scheduled. This is routinely avoided. All clients and their attorneys receive a schedule for Day 3.

Question: How does the team respond to the controversy of tests for sale on E-Bay now?

Answer: In forming an opinion, extensive interviews are relied on by both team members in lieu of personality tests results for adults. The psychologist team member is given additional time to monitor tests and screening of testing knowledge occurs in a variety of ways.

Question: What ethical guidelines have you developed unique to team evaluations?

Answer: Both team members not only follow their disciplines' guidelines, including child custody ethical conduct, but in addition, team members meet with every client seen by the other teammate. Members also create a separate report based on their own work. The team avoids basing opinions on adult testing batteries.

Bibliography

Achenbach, T., Achenbach System of Empirically Based Assessment (ASEBA) Burlington, Vermont (2007 Edition).

Amato, P. R. (2000). The consequences of divorce for adults and children. *Journal of Marriage and the Family, 62, pp.*1269–1287.

American Academy of Psychiatry and the Law (2005). *Ethics guidelines for the practice of forensic psychiatry.* Washington, DC: American Psychiatric Association.

American Psychiatric Association (2000). *The DSM IV-TR.* Washington, DC.

American Psychological Association (1994). Guidelines for child custody evaluations in divorce proceedings. *American Psychologist, 49* (7), pp. 677–680.

Association of Family and Conciliation Courts, Model standards of practice for child custody evaluation (2006), p. 18-19.

Atkinson, J. (2000). *Modern child custody practice.* 2nd ed. New York: LexisNexis.

Bennett, B. E., et al. (2006). *Assessing and managing risk in psychological practice: An individualized approach.* Rockville, MD: Trust.

Braver, S. L., Ellman, I.M., & Fabricus, W. V. (2003). Relocation of children after divorce and children's best interests: New evidence and legal considerations *Journal of Family Psychology, 17* (2), pp. 206–219.

Brown, C. (1995). Custody evaluations: Presenting the data to court. *Family and Conciliation Courts Review, 33* (4), pp. 446–461.

Bushard, P., & Howard, D. (1995). Model standards of practice for child custody evaluations. In *AFCC Resource guide for custody evaluators: A handbook for parenting evaluations.* 2nd ed. Madison, WI: Association of Family and Conciliation Courts.

Carter, B. & McGoldrick, M. (Eds.). (1988) *The changing family life cycle: A framework for family therapy.* 2nd ed. New York: Gardner Press.

Coleman, J.C. (1976) 5th Ed., *Abnormal psychology and modern life,* Glenview, IL., Scott, Foresman

Committee on Ethical Guidelines for Forensic Psychologists (1991). Specialty guidelines for forensic psychologists. *Law and Human Behavior, 6,* pp. 655–665.

Deed, M. L. (1991). Court-ordered child custody evaluations: Helping or victimizing vulnerable families. *Psychotherapy, 28,* pp. 76–84.

Ewing, C. P. (Ed.). (1991, Autumn). Divorce and child custody [Special issue]. *Behavioral Sciences and the Law,* 9 (4).

Friedman, P. H. (1987). The foundation for well-being: The care principles of well-being. *Pennsylvania Psychologist,* 6 (2), pp. 10–11.

Gottman, J. (1993). *Why marriages succeed or fail.* New York: Simon and Schuster.

Johnston, J. (1995). Children's adjustment in sole custody compared to joint custody families and principles for custody decision making. *Family and Conciliation Courts Review,* 33 (4), pp. 415–425.

Johnston, J. R., & Campbell, L. E. G. (1993). Parent-child relationships in domestic violence families disputing custody. *Family and Conciliation Courts Review,* 31 (3), pp. 282–298.

Kelly, J. B., & Lamb, E. (2003). Developmental issues in relocation cases involving young children: When, whether, and how? *Journal of Family Psychology,* 17, pp. 193–205.

Langelier, P. (1989) *The evaluation of grandparent visitation: A psychological perspective.* In Grandparent Visitation Disputes, Siegal, E., Karp, N., Editors, National Legal Resource Center for Child Advocacy and Protection Commission on Legal Problems of the Elderly, ABA Washington, DC

Langelier, Pamela (1992, Fall). Guidelines for custody evaluations. In *Family law notebook.* Reno, NV: National College of Juvenile and Family Law.

McDonalds, R. & Associates, Inc. (USDHHS) The U.S. Children's Bureau National Center on Abuse and Neglect Data Statistics, 2007, p. 184.

Melton, G. B., Petrila, J., Polythress, N. G., & Slobogin, C. (2007). *Psychological evaluations for the courts: A handbook for mental health professionals and lawyers.* 3rd ed., Chapter 16, New York, Guilford Press.

National Institute of Justice (2000). *When The Victim Is A Child.* 3rd ed. Washington, DC.

New York Times Newspaper, Stone, Brad, The Electronic Media in Child Custody Disputes, September 15, 2007.

Ollendick, D. G., & Otto, B. J. (1983). *MMPI* characteristics of parents referred for child custody studies. *Journal of Psychology, 117,* pp. 227–232.

Otto, R. & Heilbrun, K. (2002). The Practice of Forensic Psychology: A Look Toward the Future in Light of the Past. *American Psychologist, 57,* pp. 5–18.

Pope, K., Butcher, J., & Seelen, J. (2006). *The MMPI, MMPI-S, and MMPI-A in court: A practical guide for expert witnesses and attorneys.* Washington, DC: American Psychological Association.

Rakel, R. E .(2001). *Textbook of family practice* 6th ed. Philadelphia: W.B. Saunders.

Sgroi, S. M. (1995). *The handbook of clinical intervention in child sexual abuse.* 2nd ed. New York: Free Press.

Spies, R. A., Plake, B. A., eds. (2005). All Past Editions of Buros Mental Measurement Yearbook Website www.unl.edu/buros/bimm/html/catalog.html.

Stahl, P. M. (1994). *Conducting child custody evaluations: A comprehensive guide.* Thousand Oaks, CA: Sage Press.

Taylor, A., & Bing, H. (1994). Settlement by evaluation and arbitration: A new approach for custody and visitation disputes. *Family and Conciliation Courts Review, 32* (4), pp. 432–444.

Vermont Statutes Annotated (*VSA*: n.d.). Rights and responsibilities order: Best interests of the child. 15 *VSA*, Section 2, §665, pp.1667–1668.

Uniform Marriage and Divorce Act § 402, 9A, U.L.A. 561 (1987).

US Census Bureau on Divorce Statistics, 2005

Walsh, F. (1988). The family in later life. In Betty Carter & Monica McGoldrick (Eds.), *The changing family life cycle: A framework for family therapy.* 2nd ed. (pp. 311–332). New York: Gardner Press.

Warshak, R. A. (2000). Social science and children's best interests in relocation cases: Burgess revisited. *Family Law Quarterly,* 34, pp. 83–113.

Dr. Pamela Langelier has been in clinical practice for 35 years and has given international papers and hundreds of invited lectures across the country on child custody, abuse, neglect, domestic violence and on judicial decision making. She has authored numerous journal articles, book chapters and judicial training publications. Recently she co-authored with Dr. Regis Langelier, "French Canadian Families", in Ethnicity and Family Therapy, Mcgoldrick, M., Editor, Guilford Press.

She was honored with an award for A Decade of Judicial Education by the National Council of Juvenile and Family Court Judges and dedicates this publication to them.

Dr. Langelier, for the past 5 years, is a part-time Clinical Associate Professor of Family Medicine at The University of New England, Biddeford, Maine and is a principal of Langelier, Inc. a private psychology practice. She is a volunteer and mentor for homeless children at Casa de los Ninos and Aviva Children Services, Tucson, AZ.